MW00399315

ADVANCE PRAISE

"This book is a must read for online entrepreneurs. The EXITpreneur's Playbook provides powerful, clear, and easy-to-read information to help you understand the value of your most valuable asset, your business."

—GINO WICKMAN, AUTHOR OF *TRACTION* AND *ENTREPRENEURIAL LEAP*

"The EXITpreneur's Playbook is THE ULTIMATE GUIDE to selling an online business. We all need to transition our businesses someday, and those that learn from this book will have a smoother experience, an improved deal structure, and a stronger bank account."

—WALKER DEIBEL, BEST-SELLING AUTHOR OF *BUY THEN BUILD*

"The EXITpreneur's Playbook is a glimpse inside the mind of someone who has touched nearly a half billion dollars in online exits. Joe knows his stuff—and that 'stuff' is now all shared in The EXITpreneur's Playbook. If you want to maximize your exit and do it with as little pain as possible—read the book!"

—SHAKIL PRASLA, PARTNER, SZVENTURES

"*The concepts and ideas around selling an online business can be confusing and overwhelming. In The EXITpreneur's Playbook Joe has taken his knowledge and expertise and translated it into a format we can all understand—and refer back to as needed. Joe is an entrepreneur first and foremost—and speaks our language!*"

—EZRA FIRESTONE, CEO OF ZIPIFY APPS AND BOOM!
BY CINDY JOSEPH, FOUNDER OF SMART MARKETER

"*The EXITpreneur's Playbook lays out what I've seen Joe do for numerous entrepreneurs who have sold their business through his firm. In an industry where finding experienced and trusted help (and the right information) can be difficult, Joe is a refreshingly capable exception, and The EXITpreneur's Playbook demystifies what online exits entail.*"

—ANDREW YOUDERIAN, FOUNDER, ECOMMERCEFUEL

"*The EXITpreneur's Playbook will open your eyes to what it truly takes to prepare and sell a business faster and for more money. When Joe is talking, listen and TAKE ACTION on what he says. You will make more money.*"

—SCOTT VOELKER, FOUNDER AND HOST OF
THE *ROCK YOUR BRAND* PODCAST

"*Joe was part bartender, part business coach, and part friend while helping me sell my business last year. I simply couldn't imagine selling an e-commerce business with anyone else.*"

—MIKE JACKNESS, HOST OF THE *ECOMCREW* PODCAST

"*Joe helped me sell several businesses. His approach is seamless and his knowledge of the industry is unparalleled.*"

—SYED BALKHI, FOUNDER, AWESOME MOTIVE

THE

EXITPRENEUR'S

PLAYBOOK

HOW TO SELL YOUR ONLINE BUSINESS
FOR TOP DOLLAR BY
**REVERSE ENGINEERING
YOUR PATHWAY TO SUCCESS**

JOE VALLEY

LIONCREST

PUBLISHING

THE EXITPRENEUR'S PLAYBOOK
How to Sell Your Online Business for Top Dollar by Reverse Engineering Your Pathway to Success

ISBN   978-1-5445-1430-7 *Paperback*
        978-1-5445-1429-1 *Ebook*

To my wife and two boys...thank you for your love, patience, advice, and sense of humor.

CONTENTS

PART IV: THE BIG WIN

"Every wall is a door" was written by Ralph Waldo Emerson. For an EXITpreneur, this implies that for each impediment we encounter, we always find a way through, over, or beyond it. There is nothing that we cannot overcome as we progress toward our goals.

Go to EXITpreneur.io to get bonus materials, access additional resources, watch expert interviews, join the private community, and more.

FOREWORD

BY SAM PARR

When I was on the Gary Vaynerchuk podcast last year, we talked about my first real business. It was a hot dog stand called Southern Sam's Wieners as Big as Baby's Arm.

I loved that business. It was fun, put $100 to $1000 cash in my pocket daily, and connected me directly with customers. And looking back, I could have blown it up and made a ton of dough. Did I sell it? No. Should I have? Yes. Did it occur to me that I could have sold it? Absolutely not.

Regardless, that hot dog stand did something big for me: showed me that the entrepreneurial life was for me. So, after shutting it down in 2012 I left school in Nashville, Tennessee, and moved to Silicon Valley to start an internet business. I hustled, wasn't shy about meeting influencers, and eventually became one myself.

Since then, I started *The Hustle*, a business and tech newsletter with close to two million readers a day. Through my latest venture, Trends, we have tens of thousands of entrepreneurs sharing ideas on a daily basis through a private forum.

These entrepreneurs learn from each other's successes and failures. The world we live in today allows them to meet, connect, and share ideas without leaving the comfort of their homes, the office, or the local coffee shop.

They've learned that their businesses are valuable. Not just for the cash flow and freedom, but for the eventual exit.

Over the years, I've learned that one of the keys to success in life is to help others first. And that's what Joe Valley does on a daily basis.

I met Joe through a good friend of mine who sold his last business for close to eight figures with Joe as his Advisor.

It was a wild ride that helped a single dad and immigrant without a formal education put more money in the bank than most people earn in ten lifetimes. Today he's onto a new venture that he plans to sell for a billion dollars. Yes, a billion.

My friend is the perfect example of what this book is about.

He didn't go to grad school at Wharton. Didn't attend Harvard. He's like most of us. He hustles, asks questions, faces his fears daily, and reverse engineers a pathway to his goals.

Yes, he sets goals, and they are big. But they didn't start out that way. His first exit was less than $10,000—and back then (less than seven years ago) it was a fortune for a single father living month to month.

From his success I met Joe, and Joe's become one of my trusted Advisors over the years.

I often get offers for one of my businesses, and the first thing I do is call Joe for his advice, wisdom, and experience. I always walk away with a new perspective or something I hadn't thought of, and everything he says is always in my best interest.

Since selling his last online business in 2010, Joe has turned his focus to helping entrepreneurs understand the value of their own businesses. He's had his hands in nearly a half billion in exits through Quiet Light—a firm he and his partner run to help online entrepreneurs understand the value of what they have, and then exit at a time and value that is right for them.

Joe is a sought-after speaker, podcaster (and guest), and guest in mastermind groups and Ask Me Anythings (AMAs). And he's had thousands of one-on-one conversations with online entrepreneurs. He tailors each conversation to that person and their business. He admits it's a delicate, detailed, and creative process—and that thousands more who need to hear what he has to say are being left out.

That's why he wrote *The EXITpreneur's Playbook*. Everything he's learned in the last decade about online exits is in the book. And as boring as the topic of "exits" can be, Joe's voice comes through as clear as if you were having a beer with him at your favorite pub.

It's filled with real-life examples of his own, and his clients', successes and failures. It provides exactly what entrepreneurs need: knowledge in layman's terms about the value of their most important—and likely most valuable—asset: their business.

Odds are you know the value of your house, car, or retirement funds. But what about your business?

Through sheer force of will and a little luck, you are a successful entrepreneur. Your business is worth something—no matter the size. Learn the value of what you have, but don't go it alone. Get real advice, real tools, and real inspiration.

The EXITpreneur's Playbook is the definitive guide to selling online businesses. Read it, refer back to it, and share it—and you'll find that the best days get better, the tough days are shrugged off, and an eventual exit of your business for the value you want, when you want, with the deal structure you want, is in your future.

INTRODUCTION

Like a good story, there are two sides to every business sale—plus the guy in the middle, which is where I can be found these days. But I've been on the buying and selling sides of my own business deals too. I've also been on the losing-way-too-much-money side, the what-the-hell-have-I-done side, and the thankfully-this-advisor-is-helping-me side.

From my own business startups, acquisitions, and exits to the hundreds that I've helped facilitate over the last nine years, one thing remains true:

In most cases, more than 50 percent of all the money you'll ever make from your business comes on the day you sell it.

In fact: *If your business is less than thirty-six months old and growing rapidly, the percentage is much higher.*

And for an EXITpreneur? Well, the next incredible exit is just around the corner.

So, what is an EXITpreneur? The simple answer is an entrepreneur *with knowledge and a plan.*

An EXITpreneur understands the real dollar value of their business is likely in the exit. They also know who they are in life and business and won't make the mistake of letting a business outgrow them, trapping them in something they don't enjoy. They'll sell first, and then move on to their next adventure.

In other words, they have a plan to capture the financial worth and fruits of their labor. They have a plan to live the lifestyle of their choosing. The EXITpreneur understands that no one really owns a business forever. They have a plan in advance of the inevitable end, so they can make the most of the transition from one owner to the next, for the good of both parties.

You don't like planning? Welcome to the club. Not many entrepreneurs love this work, so think of it as training instead.

If you want to compete in a triathlon, run a marathon, or even take on a 5K, you have to train. A successful exit is not simply a matter of wanting it—it's a matter of training and of making everyday choices that will prepare you for the big day. I'm here to help you with your training. This is your playbook, but it's up to you to put it in action.

FROM OWNER TO SELLER TO EXITPRENEUR

Jeremy started out in the corporate world, but found that it didn't give him the kind of life he wanted to live. He and his wife, a teacher, had a young child, and they began talking about what they could do to change the trajectory of his career. With her great benefits and steady income as their anchor, they decided to launch an e-commerce business. Jeremy left his six-figure salary to be a stay-at-home dad while running the business, with the ultimate goal of selling the business once it was ready.

He reached out to me with his goals about twelve months in, and we reverse engineered a path to achieve them.

Jeremy and his wife bootstrapped their business with a home equity line of credit, then invested deeper later on to keep up with inventory. They never took a penny in salary from the profits. For twenty-four months, they lived solely on his wife's teacher salary, which we all know isn't much. Every ounce of profit went back into inventory and the growth of the business, with the sole exception of a $600 camera for product shots that he kept after he sold.

After two years of coming and going as he pleased, being around for his wife and son, and driving the business forward until it became attractive to buyers, Jeremy was ready to list his business. Because he had planned well from the beginning— outsourced his bookkeeping, kept his numbers in order, and created something a buyer would love to take over—his million-dollar sale was closed within forty-five days.

Doing the math, that means Jeremy left his stressful six-figure job and replaced it with earnings of half a million a year, complete freedom, lower tax rates, and solid experience that will allow him to do it all over again when he's ready.

In another part of the country, Leigh emigrated from Vietnam to the US with her mother and sisters when she was just fifteen years old. Her mother had $200 to her name, and none of the family spoke any English. Yet they all were gifted with an incredible work ethic that drove them to not only survive, but to thrive and adapt in a completely foreign environment.

Leigh launched an online business with two brands that both

took off. She reached out to me at the beginning of 2018 when her husband was going to be relocated to Japan, hoping to sell the business so that they could move on with this new phase of life. Her business wasn't perfect—the manufacturing wasn't streamlined, a lot of her products had to be purchased locally in San Francisco, and we weren't sure how that would work for a new buyer. For about three weeks, a lot of buyers showed interest in her listing. However, with the business to run and a new baby to care for, the selling process became a massive source of stress for her.

One day she called me to say she had to pull the plug. Her husband's transfer fell through, so the urgency to sell was gone, and she wanted to wait a little longer until the conditions of her business and personal life were a little more favorable.

It was a tough call for Leigh to make. Buyers had put time into their inquiries. Relationships had been built. I'd put time into it too, but I'm never going to force someone into a sale when they're not ready. It was her business and her call to make. We pulled the listing and formed a plan to make her business even more streamlined and attractive for buyers when the time came.

Fifteen months later, she came back, ready to go. The business was much stronger, and her manufacturing issues had been sorted out. We listed it for 40 percent more than we had the first time, and because she had grown it with the next buyer in mind, people were willing to pay a higher multiple for it. Less than twenty years after coming to this country with no money and no English skills, Leigh sold her business for almost three-quarters of a million dollars.

Then there's Paul. A buttoned-up CPA working for a firm in his field, Paul came to me in his late twenties with a twelve-month-old business he was planning to sell.

One winter, he and his wife had fled the North to visit his parents down in Phoenix. During that trip, he watched and learned as his parents and their friends played a strange new game that he'd never seen before. The more he learned, the more he saw a niche market opportunity in the works. He did his homework and found that there wasn't much competition for this game online. Unhappy with his existing career, he and his wife decided to save up some money and launch a brand within that niche.

Paul built the business the right way from the beginning. He and his wife already had some experience selling online, so they knew how to get it off on the right foot. He made sure not to commingle this brand with anything else they had done, which allowed the sale to qualify for a small business administration (SBA) loan. And even though he was a CPA, he outsourced the day-to-day bookkeeping to an e-commerce bookkeeper. When the time came to sell, about thirty months after the launch, his numbers were perfect and the buyers were confident in both the business and Paul.

The beautiful thing about Paul's story is just how humble he stayed from beginning to end. In fact, I wanted to launch the listing at a higher price than what we went with, but Paul was just ready to get it done.

In the video interviews that we always post with our listings, Paul was so honest, sincere, and likable that hundreds of buyers were interested right away. The response was incredible. He demonstrated the product and met with the first fifteen qualified buyers to request conference calls, and within the first two weeks he had ten offers. In a surprise reward for his care and concern for the next owners, one of the offers was a couple hundred thousand dollars over asking—and that's not even the buyer that Paul chose.

Then there's Victor, who has worked through the EXITpreneur's playbook like a pro, even before it was written. With a history that includes homelessness as a teen and construction work as a young adult, he eventually discovered affiliate marketing and the potential to build and sell a content site.

His first exit came in at just $7,500, and with the lessons he learned from that sale, he bought another business and did it again. The second one sold for $20,000. After that he bought and optimized another content site. After letting it age and grow a bit, he sold that one for $220,000. By now it is obvious that Victor is clearly learning the ways of the EXITpreneur. Within twenty-four months, Victor was back with another business he was ready to sell. That one sold for just under $9 million and his life has changed forever. He's not done though. I interviewed Victor while writing this book and he's shooting for another exit in the next few years—it's a lofty goal of a billion-dollar exit. Knowing him…he'll achieve it!

The one thing each of these incredible exits has in common is this: the process of selling was an integral part of their business plan and vision from early on.

TRAIN FOR AN EXIT OR EXPECT TO FAIL

I've helped business owners reach their goals and make incredible exits happen from as low as fifty grand up to eight figures, with each sale as unique to the seller as their business is in the world.

I've also watched way too many of the people who come to me say, "I got this," and disappear into oblivion. As a good friend of mine says, "Most entrepreneurs are just trying to keep the wheels on the bus and not run out of money." They don't want to think about the planning and the numbers and the structure that the next owner will need. Sometimes, they don't even want to think past the next round of code development or inventory orders. They don't want to get serious about what a sale requires until they're ready for it to happen, which unfortunately means the ideal sale won't happen at all. Not like it could have. Not like an EXITpreneur would make it happen.

Here's the hard truth: if your business doesn't die out first, eventually someone else is going to take it over. You'll pass it on to your kids, competitors will swoop in, or you'll get so burned out that you'll have to make something happen, but it won't be ideal.

If you haven't planned for an exit that hands off a *great business* to a *great buyer* for a *great price*, an inevitable end is going to find you anyway, and it'll catch you off guard when it does.

The stories of incredible exits that I share in this book aren't about branding or products or marketing. The stories are about the vision entrepreneurs had for the future. They're about the preparation they made to offset risk, document impeccably, and create a fully transferable business with clear paths to growth for the next owner.

The EXITpreneur understands that true wealth is built when they sell, so that's where their goals are set. They know who they are as entrepreneurs and will never let the business outgrow their passion, capabilities, or attention span. Once their financial exit goal is defined, they learn how the math really works to value a business, find out what buyers in their niche really want, and then chart a clear and defined path toward their goals.

Yes, they reverse engineer their pathway to success.

Those clearly defined plans help you keep going when things get tough—and at some point, or another, they always get tough.

Jeremy, Victor, Leigh, and Paul chose the path of knowledge, planning, and training with an eye on the ultimate prize. They created businesses that someone would be happy to take over, and they were paid handsomely for their efforts.

BIG MIKE AND JIMMY: TWO CAUTIONARY TALES

My first million-dollar listing was for a guy we'll call Big Mike. I knew his financials were nonexistent, but I was a relatively new Advisor who wanted to make it work anyway. I did everything I could to help him get his profit and loss statements (P&Ls) in great shape. I suggested that he hire an experienced e-commerce bookkeeper to assist him with the financials, but Big Mike didn't want to. Unfortunately, I wasn't savvy enough to send him away until he was ready. I was eager and hopeful and wanted to help those who couldn't help themselves.

Big Mike certainly could not and would not help himself.

That year, I spent Christmas break entering his bank statements and vendor invoices into a P&L Excel file going back three years.

We listed his business for $1.1 million and, because the numbers were trailing down in a niche industry in need of innovation, he got an $800,000 offer. Our team thought it was a fair offer, and I was proud of my work to get even that much.

Big Mike was not impressed. He had stars in his eyes about the energy he could put into a pay per click (PPC) marketing campaign and decided to push toward some ROI goals for another twenty-four months.

The math and logic made sense, so I helped him tighten up his plan, advised him again to hire an e-commerce bookkeeper, and sent him on his way.

Six months later, he called back ready to try again. Except he hadn't implemented the plans and he hadn't hired a bookkeeper. Instead of $800,000, the updated trends and data said the best he might get for the business was $600,000. Back to the drawing board he went.

Tragically, this pattern has repeated for the last five years. Every year, Big Mike comes to me with hopes to sell, and every year I have to deliver the bad news that the value still isn't where he wants it to be. His personal expenses are so high that he's pulling every ounce of cash from the business that he can, instead of putting it into growth. To make matters worse, his competitors have made the niche into something he doesn't want to do anymore. He's still got the business, but he's had to do other things for income on top of it because it can't support him and his family.

That $800,000 that he turned down would have allowed him to pay off debt and move forward with experience, passion, and drive for another adventure. Instead, he refused the pain of investing in help. He refused the pain of detailed paperwork. He refused the pain of a lower realistic value and the pain of cutting his personal overhead for the sake of the business. Now he's stuck with the pain of a business he doesn't want, at a value that will never recover. He chose the wrong pain.

CHOOSE YOUR PAIN

The expression "choose your pain" is not my creation. It comes from a trainer at beachbody.com.

I first heard it when I was five minutes into a grueling thirty-minute workout, when the trainer yelled out something like, "Toughen up and choose the right pain! Choose the pain of training and working out—or choose the pain of doing nothing, being unhealthy, and unable to do the things you love."

Truer words have never been spoken!

I desperately wanted to help Big Mike—and I still do—but I can't do anything about expectations that are not in line with reality.

Since then, I've learned to choose my own pain. The hardest part of my role comes when I have to tell an excited business owner that it's not going to work. In some ways, it's even harder than digging through bank statements on Christmas Eve. This was the case for Jimmy.

Jimmy came to me with $10 million a year in revenue and an initial business valuation of $6 to 7 million. At first glance, his business had plenty of potential. Once the deep dive into the financials started, however, the flaws began to emerge.

First, I noticed that Jimmy had used a cash-based accounting method rather than accrual. If you aren't familiar with those terms and the significance they carry, I'll explain them later in the book. For now, it's enough to know that we had to change that around.

I thought Jimmy had simply run the wrong report, but when I asked for an accrual-based P&L, he couldn't provide one. (In fact, most people can't—that's okay. We'll cover that later too.) He was spending $24,000 a year on an entry-level bookkeeper who had no idea how to make the adjustments. And it got worse.

On a video call with Jimmy while we tried to sort the accounting numbers out, he pointed out a number I was sharing from my screen.

"What's that?" he asked. "I didn't do $297,000 in July. There's no way."

"Jimmy," I tried to gently remind him, "those numbers came from your P&L."

He found the discrepancy, but it shed light on the biggest problem he had: there's no way to sell a business with numbers that are wrong.

Turns out, there was a half-million-dollar bottom-line discrepancy between reality and what the original bookkeeper had presented. His business was worth $3 million at best—less than half of what he thought it was going to be.

Jimmy hadn't done his homework. He hadn't paid attention to the numbers. He hadn't hired the right people and didn't understand how to prepare a business to hand over to someone else. The worst part of it all is that he wasted money doing it. For about half the money, he could have hired an e-commerce bookkeeping firm to replace the $24,000 salary of the person who did it wrong. That's a $12,000 gap. At a 4x multiple of Seller's Discretionary Earnings (SDE) (we'll cover this later, too), that turns into $48,000 added to the list price of his business, not to mention getting the value where it should have been in the first place.

Listen, I fell asleep in accounting class. Literally. I don't love doing that kind of work either. But a basic understanding of the numbers is critical if you're going to build this kind of wealth.

Sometimes, when the truth is ugly and the work is hard, you can tell whether you're talking to an EXITpreneur or a burned-out entrepreneur. Their eyes glaze over. They're emotionally spent, and they've got no heart left to rally for change. The later in the game an exit comes into view, the harder it is to get and keep control of it.

Jimmy is a great guy, and I hope to hear from him again. I would love to hear that he went back and shifted his expectations, chose the painful work that will pay off in the long run, and salvaged what he could out of a bad situation. He has the tools, resources, referrals, and data to make it work and have an incredible exit of his own. He does have a great business and just needs to clean up his numbers to get the value right and instill confidence in buyers.

Now, contrast Big Mike and Jimmy with Syed, a business owner who is prepared for an eventual sale from the moment he starts a business. Syed is always ready to exit when the time is right. For each brand, he sets up a separate LLC, with separate accounting, documentation, and staffing or billable hours. He runs a massive WordPress plugin business, and I helped him sell three of his other smaller businesses. Two are Software as a Service (SaaS) businesses and one is a content site. Each time, they've been SBA eligible, with plenty of offers on the table (both cash and SBA buyers). Why? Because Syed consistently chooses the pain of logistics for the payoff of an incredible exit. He cares about his businesses and the future owner who will take over for him, and when he's ready to move on, it's a breeze. He's an EXITpreneur, through and through.

HOW TO USE THIS PLAYBOOK

Everything you're about to read has come out of my mouth thousands of times in personal conversations and public venues. Yet I still get asked about the same things over and over again. Sometimes from the same people. Sometimes within the same conversation.

The way we put listing packages together at Quiet Light isn't rocket science. It's hard work that we've done so many times that it comes naturally. For everyone else, it's like a foreign language—the very language I'll teach you in this book.

The more times you see and hear and feel and talk about the nature of an exit, the more ingrained that process will become. I want you to know what it takes to sell a business, inside and out, upside and down, so that it becomes part of your business strategy from its earliest stages. I want you to set a target value and reverse engineer that value into every decision you make.

I want you to run your business so well that the exit is the best part, not a reluctant end. I want the next owners of your business to be thrilled to start from a solid foundation and grow it to new heights.

I want you to do better than Big Mike and Jimmy and even me. I want you to do better with your next sale than you did on your last, and even better the time after that.

I want you to know more, do better, sell bigger, and excitedly move on to your next adventure, whether that is another business, charity work, or your golf swing.

There's an indescribable, insurmountable level of emotional and financial pain that comes when you wait until the end to plan for a sale. In the pages to come, I'll tell you stories of people who avoided that pain and others who succumbed to it. I'll walk you through everything I know about valuations, risks, and viable businesses. I'll show you how to set your intentions and do the work required of an EXITpreneur, so that you can create the incredible outcomes that EXITpreneurs have.

This is your playbook, and your training begins now. Whether you put it into action is up to you.

PART I

GAME PLAN: EXIT WELL

CHAPTER 1

EYES ON THE PRIZE

If I knew anything about it back when I was selling my first business, I would have been an original EXITpreneur. I could have known myself better, set my business up for the next owner, and watched for the right time to sell—both from a market standpoint and my own interest level. I would have moved on earlier, instead of holding the company back when the next steps fell outside of my comfort zone. But I thought I was just an entrepreneur, and I thought that entrepreneurs were supposed to hold onto their creations until the bitter end.

Owning a business was my inevitable path in life. I had the childhood many business owners can relate to—mowing lawns and running paper routes and finding ways to make some extra cash wherever I could. I was always working on something bigger, too, like the worm farm my dad let me set up in the basement in junior high. Since we lived on one of the central streets in our town in Maine, a "Nightcrawlers for Sale" sign out front brought fishermen knocking on the door looking for bait. I'd bag them up, then go out with a flashlight at night to find more to replenish my stash. My muddy grasp on supply and demand opportunities started young and never left me alone.

I did attempt to take other routes. During my undergrad at Northeastern University, I participated in a co-op program that split the year's work between school and on-the-job experience. For the first nine months, I tried my hand at corporate life. I can't lie—I felt like a big shot with my secondhand-store suit and briefcase filled only with lunch. But as soon as I realized I was just a cog in a wheel, I was done. It was going to take more than the allure of money to hold my interest.

For a little while, working as an assistant manager for an upstart fast food franchise scratched the itch.[1] When the twenty-something-year-old who hired me asked, "Do you like beer?" during the interview, I was immediately hooked on small business life. The corporate world this was not. We worked hard and played hard, and that was all there was to it. I loved it for what it was, and kept my eyes open for what might be next. That opportunity looked like a guy named Michael Hackel, wearing a beat-up leather jacket, jeans, and an Oxford dress shirt and carrying an old leather briefcase, hoping to get our restaurant on board with his restaurant delivery service.

The idea was simple, but for a Cajun fast food restaurant in the late '80s, it was revolutionary: customers wanted food delivered, and restaurants weren't doing it. Michael's company—DiningIn—would keep menus for any of their participating restaurants, take the order over the phone, fax the order to the restaurant, then pick up and deliver the food. After Michael made his sales pitch and left, I told the co-owner I wanted in. More specifically, I told him I wanted to do it *myself*. The entrepreneur in me couldn't resist a good opportunity. He thought it

---

1   Fun side note: The restaurant was called Cajun Joe's Fried Chicken and Biscuits, and eventually the owners sold it to Subway. At one point, the founder of Subway, Fred Deluca, was in our little band of restaurants and I got to say hello and shake his hand.

was a smart enough idea and offered some backing if I wanted to give it a shot. We shook hands and became fifty-fifty partners on the spot.

Michael's model had been carefully built, modified, and branded for high-end restaurants—all of his drivers wore tuxedos and made it feel like "dining in" a fancy restaurant.

Mine was named during a brainstorming session with a roommate, another roommate's girlfriend, and the assistance of a smokable herb that is now legal in most states in the US. We came up with "The Wrong Number," because how *funny* would it be to answer the phone and say "wrong number" when it wasn't wrong? (I know—not so bright.)

Needless to say, we weren't going to encroach on Michael's high-end market. We stuck to the foods that college kids wanted delivered, and within a week I had five restaurants on board. Why? There was a real need for the service, and it removed all of the pain points for the restaurant owners. I also hustled and just knew the idea made sense. Even with a dumb name.

I launched The Wrong Number while maintaining my full-time student status at Northeastern. I worked eight to ten hours a night, seven nights a week, for months, and somehow didn't let my grades suffer. It was a blast.

Clearly, between the name and the workload, I wasn't thinking about the eventual exit. I kept the business going for nearly six months, then quit after Christmas break. I quickly learned that lifestyle is important to me, and I had no intention of working that much for however many years it would take to make The Wrong Number worthwhile.

Not too long after closing up shop I applied for and became a driver for DiningIn. I was still a kid, a student, and an eventual entrepreneur. I made more money as a driver than as an owner. But I knew I'd still run my own business someday.

After I graduated and moved on, I watched from a distance and learned as Michael grew the business, invested in technology, expanded to other cities, and eventually exited well to a company that we would all come to know and love—Grubhub.

In the years that followed, I kicked around in the corporate world again, played with a couple of business ideas, and even tried to be a brick-and-mortar business broker for a little while. Each new venture taught me a little more about what I did and didn't want. None of them felt quite right and it was great to narrow things down by process of elimination.

On a cold Saturday in January of 1994, I finally hit it off with another interviewer who was young, hip, and pretty casual. It was a Saturday—moving day for the company—and the person who hired me was wearing sweats! I had my ten-cent suit on, bought at the Buffalo Exchange in San Francisco a few months back, and I became employee number thirty-four.

I loved the small-but-rapidly-growing entrepreneurial atmosphere at that company. As we grew from $17 million in revenue in 1994 to $101 million in 1997, my role was always changing, from sales rep to manager to media buyer. But the more the company grew, the more restrictive the environment became. I stayed until the company fully outgrew me, which, to be completely transparent, looked like me trying to resign but getting let go instead, complete with the head of HR escorting me out the door.

This was exactly what I needed. Within a few weeks, I had opened my own radio-based direct response media-buying agency. I was finally settling in as an entrepreneur, where it seemed I was always going to be. However, just like in college, I worked forty-plus hours a week as a sales rep for a call center nights and weekends while launching and building my media-buying business during the day.

Over the next fifteen years, there were plenty of ups and downs and lessons to be learned—some of which I'll cover in the next chapter, and some of which can only properly be told over a beer. The bottom line is that I survived, thrived, and evolved. My business morphed from traditional media buying to launching my own brands on radio and television, producing two TV infomercials, co-hosting one, and ultimately moving to a 100 percent online business model in 2005.

I ran my e-commerce business through the best and worst of the economy. And I emerged on the other side—more tired than victorious. In 2010, I woke up one morning and decided I would sell. No planning, no prep work. I was bored, I was done, and I wanted out right then.

Years later, when refining the EXITpreneur process, I realized we had to differentiate between *deciding* to sell a business and *planning* to sell it. Because far too many people decide to sell like I did, when a plan could have ensured their success.

An EXITpreneur doesn't have to set a timeframe when, ready or not, it's time to sell. But most entrepreneurs will eventually want out one day, whether or not the business is ready. Planning for that day from the start (or from wherever you are in this moment) can set you up for fewer headaches and a greater chance at success.

Planning to exit is about realistic expectations. It's knowing that the time will come to move on, even if you don't know exactly when that will happen. It's creating the underlying structure that allows you to sell then, instead of waiting until you're emotionally spent. By that point, the window to exit well has probably closed.

My exit from my e-commerce business was years too late. The signs had all been there. Well before the financial crisis hit, I had emotionally checked out. I wasn't interested in the details anymore, and my disconnect began to take its toll. Had I planned then—better yet, trained and gained knowledge from the beginning—I could have passed it along to a buyer with more energy and passion. Who knows where they could have taken it. Who knows what I could have done differently had I envisioned an incredible potential exit and the many more that could have followed.

Here's the upside: because I learned the hard way, you don't have to.

TRAINING FOR YOUR EXIT

Selling a business is, not surprisingly, mostly about the numbers. I'm not going to hold back on the accounting details and math equations that will make your eventual exit make sense, so steel yourself now. But before we get to all of that, let's start with the simplest and most exciting number to remember: most business owners make *at least 50 percent* of all the money they'll ever make from their business on the day they sell.

I mentioned this in the introduction, but it's worth digging deeper to really understand. That percentage reflects *all* of the income you collect, for the lifetime of the business. What you make on closing day will, in almost every case, be more than what you collected in profits and salary.

When I consult with business owners, their wheels start turning right about now. This is especially true for businesses that are less than five years old. And it does not matter if yours is a content, SaaS, or product-based business. The fact is that the costs associated with the startup phase in the first few years result in lower cash flows—making an exit the greatest source of financial reward.

As you'll learn throughout this book, online businesses are not valued on cash flows, but on Seller's Discretionary Earnings, or SDE. Some may call this adjusted earnings before interest, taxes, depreciation, and amortization (EBITDA), but the generally accepted term is SDE.

Let's say you've got a product-based business and built your cash flow up to take $150,000 a year out as income. The rest of what you make goes back into the business to fuel the beast. You do this for four years and take out $0 the first year, $50,000 the second, $100,000 the third, and $150,000 the fourth—a total of $300,000. You've got $150,000 tied up in inventory and your SDE (not cash flow) settles in around $300,000—then you sell the business for a million dollars. That means you made a total of $1.3 million, with much more than half of that coming at the point of sale.

Let's look at an example.

Owner cash flow from operations:

Year 1:	$0
Year 2:	$50,000
Year 3:	$100,000
Year 4:	$150,000
Total:	$300,000

Taxed as ordinary income you might get to keep 60–65 percent of this, depending on where you live. So let's say you've got about 65 percent of this left after taxes—or about $195,000.

You've also sold the business for $1 million at the end of year four. After capital gains taxes (about 25 percent depending again on where you live) and the Advisor fee, you are left with about $675,000 in after-tax monies.

Combined, you've pocketed about $870,000.

Did you make more money selling the business or running it?

- Sold = $675,000 after-tax money
- Operating = $195,000 after-tax money over four years

That's 3.46 times the amount of after-tax money you made in four years earned by selling. As noted above, a nice little bonus is that the proceeds from the sale are taxed as capital gains, not ordinary income. This is normally a much lower rate, allowing you to keep an extra 10–15 percent versus giving it to Uncle Sam.

The point of this metric, though, isn't to give you a hard and fast number to expect when you sell your business. There are absolutely business owners who don't plan well and wind up losing money or selling short, and there are owners who make far beyond 50 percent. The real value here is in understanding how financially significant the sale is in the life cycle of the business.

As entrepreneurs we get excited about the early stages of a business. It's a new adventure. We work hard without earning much money, and we love every minute. The more successful the business gets, the more we make, then one of two things happens: either the business needs us more than we want to give in order to get it to the next level, or it needs us less and loses its excitement.

In any case, there are very few Mark Zuckerberg unicorns out there who build the business to exponential levels and still stick around. Accepting this reality means bringing training for an exit into our growth plans. Ignoring it can be a costly, miserable mistake.

WHEN THE BUSINESS OUTGROWS YOU

Last week, I had coffee with a guy who did $7 million in revenue last year and will easily top $20 million this year. His business has also tripled its employees and is aiming to triple its revenue again next year to $60 million. He's funded with venture money and is thrilled by the responsibility of making other people's money grow. That's the kind of entrepreneur he is.

That's the kind of entrepreneur that an EXITpreneur sells to.

For most of us, we've quit our corporate jobs and started a business for the freedom of it. We never want to miss another sporting event or birthday party. We want cookouts with our families on the weekends instead of pulling another shift. But when the business hits a certain point, it becomes bigger and needier than that lifestyle can afford. It needs more than we have to give. At that point, we have a decision to make. If we hang onto it, we have to grow with the business. That requires an office and staff and HR and complexities that we may or may not be suited for.

Or, we can sell it and move on to our next adventure—an exciting, freedom-generating project, and very likely while being debt-free with plenty of money in the bank.

The key is to know yourself and be honest about what you're in business for. Some people are great with having lots of employees and managing an office, local or remote. They're great with importing, vendor management, product development, multiple channels of revenue, innovations, debt, accounts payable, and so much aspirin. The headaches are part of it for them, and that's fine.

But be honest with yourself here. Are you that person? If not and your business continues to grow, it may wind up neglected as you take your eyes off it to focus on other more interesting things, or simply because you are not good at this part or stage of a business. When the business is neglected, it trends downward and loses value rapidly. Once your energy drains out and you've emotionally left the building, your business won't sell as well as it would have. You may not get to sell it at all.

Know your limitations. Be realistic about why you're in business. Identify signals that your business might be bigger than you bargained for. Then implement your plan to exit at a time and price that suits you.

WHEN YOU GET BORED

A person who starts business after business is often referred to as a serial entrepreneur. We picture them as antsy and excitable, hopping from one great idea to the next. There is a different feeling to that kind of entrepreneurship, and not everyone feels suited to it. At the same time, there's something unrealistic about sticking with a business until it runs its course. When the newness of a startup settles down into the day to day, they lose interest.

EXITpreneurs fall somewhere in between the manic feeling of a serial entrepreneur and the trapped feeling of staying with the same business through retirement.

Now, a serial entrepreneur *can* be an EXITpreneur too—once you've bootstrapped and sold a growing business once, it's much easier to do it all over again. We'll start multiple businesses in the duration of our career, because we love it. We're not in business to stand back and let someone else run it. We're here to start new things and watch them take off.

The key is that we start each business knowing where we want to take it, and this allows us to grow it until it's time to exit, then collect that big payday at the closing table before doing it all over again.

That's the game plan in a nutshell: bootstrap, grow, sell, repeat.

Everyone is going to exit their business or role within their business at some point, whether it's after a couple of years, after a long period of management, or when it's time to pass it along to our kids. Even my friend who is growing his business toward $60 million will eventually do the same thing. He'll sell it when it's worth $250 million or so, then pick up another growing business and do it all over again. Or maybe his next adventure will be traveling, skiing, or golf—who knows. Setting goals and gaining knowledge on how to exit well will determine how smoothly and lucratively that transition is made.

Your exit—one way or another—is inevitable, so why not train for it? Why not make it incredible?

So, do you know the value of your most valuable asset? Or are you being a Jackie?

DON'T BE A "JACKIE"

In my house, you may hear the occasional "OK Jackie" or "Hey, Jackie" when someone says or does something foolish. It's not an insult to those named Jackie. No, it's simply our cute way of saying jackass—and reminding each other not to be one. Here's your reminder: don't be a Jackie!

Fortunately, the process of preparing your business for an exit is the same whether you make just under six figures or well over eight. No matter what stage your business is in or what "incredible" looks like for you, the same details will matter. The same steps will apply.

For the EXITpreneur, that process becomes ingrained as you follow it for the first sale, then the next, and the next. Some of my clients have started with tens of thousands and built up to millions. They created exits they'd only dreamed about, by taking one measured step at a time.

That's what I want for you.

I want each person of the thousands I've talked to—and then thousands more on top of that—to have every tool they need to do this the right way. I want every dream about closing day to come true. I want every business owner to picture the day they'll exit, work toward it, and make it a reality—long before the business outgrows them or fizzles into nothing or leaves them emotionally spent and no better off financially.

I want *you* to have the tools in your hand, ready to reference each time you forget what an add-back is or need to know which accounting method to use. I want you to believe in your future incredible exit so clearly that the details are worth tracking.

Unfortunately, they are still details. There's a learning curve ahead, and it's not going to be easy. But I promise, if you stick with it, it'll be worth it. Incredible, even.

THE CURIOSITY ADVANTAGE

Successful EXITpreneurs aren't just looking for the empty promise of a high valuation. They want to understand what they actually have and how to make it better. They set goals and want to learn how to reach them. They know they won't run the business forever, and they want to get it ready for the next owner. They're willing to learn and do what's necessary in order to reach an incredible exit.

EXITpreneurs are curious about every angle of their business because they understand that the exit matters as much or more than any other piece of the business.

Think of it this way: For the vast majority of people, their home is their biggest asset, and they take that knowledge seriously.

Even though For Sale By Owner is technically an option, most home sales happen via real estate professionals on one or both sides of the deal. We know what we don't know, and we don't want to take the chance that we'll get something wrong.

If we can respect the nuances of that purchase—the significance of that value in our lives—why would we downplay the valuation and sale of a business?

It still happens, unfortunately. Too many online entrepreneurs think they can avoid the expense of an Advisor by doing it themselves. Sometimes it's a symptom of the "I've got this" mentality that helped them build and run the business. Other times, they simply have the impression that it's easy—their buddy sold for a multiple of three times. Basic math. No problem.

But a business is worth more and made up of more moving parts than a home, and a multiple holds much more than surface calculations. A proper valuation is a complex process that you need to understand thoroughly or get help to do right—and usually, you need both a good understanding *and* good help.

Unfortunately, even for those who understand and appreciate the work of a business Advisor, there is a strange but real resistance around asking questions and consulting with one before you feel like you're "done" with the business. Some of it is for good reason. Bad players will do anything they need to do in order to get a business owner to sign an engagement letter to sell with them. They'll overpromise and underdeliver on valuation, then backtrack when buyers won't bite. It's unethical and dishonest, and gives the industry a bad name. Crucially, it also keeps business owners from asking good questions and getting a solid plan in place.

I began with my story as an early entrepreneur and will continue to share some of my experiences throughout the book because it's important for you to know that I'm not *just* an Advisor, or whatever you want to call me. I've been in your shoes. I've had to get my hands dirty to learn what it means to be an EXITpreneur. I've built, bought, and sold my own online businesses that changed my net worth and the path that the rest of my life would take.

In other words, my goal here isn't to turn you into a client, but an EXITpreneur. I want to turn you into someone who appreciates what you're up against and knows what's important to track and plan for.

By the end, you'll understand valuations better than your peers and some of mine. You'll understand your business better than you ever have, which means you'll be able to create a plan for your exit, whether it happens in six months or six years.

SEE YOURSELF EXITING WELL

I've spoken to thousands of curious entrepreneurs, and I find that I have to actively turn people away. Recently, someone was referred to me who is a successful entrepreneur with multiple businesses and brands, including a utility patent on one particular product. He has even been on *Shark Tank*, where he got a deal with Robert. After the show aired, the televised transaction he'd agreed to was modified, and it fell through. He kept the business for a few years after that, but now he wants out.

In this particular case, let's say he made $1 million in 2017, then $1.2 million in 2018. But in 2019, he stopped spending money on advertising and dropped to $100,000 in revenue. When I asked him why his revenue had dropped, he said, "I thought the organic ranking and the lift from the show would be all that was needed."

"Okay," I continued. "What are your exit goals—what are you hoping to sell the business for?"

"I'd like to exit at about $1.4 to 1.5 million."

Here's the catch: incredible exits come together when it's a good opportunity for the *buyer*, not just the seller—when all of the details are in place and there are clear paths to growth.

Because he waited so long and planned so poorly, the exit he envisioned isn't going to happen, regardless of the IP or his *Shark Tank* exposure. Someone has to come rescue this sinking ship of a business, and it's going to be a risk when they do. They have to bring working capital to the table and get that ad spend back up. They have to figure out what will work today, which is probably different than what worked twelve or eighteen months ago. They have to build up the brand name, the recognition, and everything else to get it going again. That will take risk and capital investment. As such, it's an unsellable business in the general marketplace, or at least unsellable at his desired price, by a longshot.

No matter how attached you are to the idea of your business, no one is going to pay you a bunch of money by pretending that you have amazing numbers that just aren't there.

Unfortunately, I have that conversation far too often. Entrepreneurs come to me ready to sell, but the business isn't sellable at a number that works for them. I try to help them and educate them and put them on the right path so they can take what they've learned, pivot, and grow their businesses to a point where they can truly exit them, hopefully for the values they want. Ultimately, whether or not they can make that happen is up to them. If you wait until you're emotionally toast, like I did back in 2010, it's going to be difficult to follow through and achieve your goals.

I'm not promising an easy alternative. There are a lot of nuances to this, and it's going to take this whole book to sort it out. But once you do—once you follow the game plan and exit well—it only gets easier. The pathway becomes clearer. The exits get more incredible. You become an EXITpreneur.

But really, you were always one to begin with, weren't you?

CHAPTER 2

NO PAIN NO GAIN

I just blew $100,000.

I knew it. Probably everyone there knew it. And I had no idea how much more I was about to lose.

I was in the production room for a TV infomercial that should have worked, except my wife and I stepped out of hosting it at the last minute. Instead, we pulled in two people who made sense on paper but did not get along at all on camera. As predicted, the infomercial bombed and I lost about $100,000 in the process.

Fortunately, there was a companion radio campaign that did well. *Un*fortunately, I got greedy and said those infamous words: "That looks easy enough. *I got this.*"

After about a year of smooth sailing and huge profits, I got frustrated with one of the owners of a call center that had been taking my radio spot ad calls and handling customer service. In order to take a bit more control and save some money, I decided to bring the customer service in-house. It turns out he was frustrated with me as well, and within a couple of weeks he gave me a thirty-day notice that they'd no longer be taking my inbound sales calls. *Oops.*

No problem, though—after all, it's just a call center, right? And there were plenty in the area that were offshoots from the previous company I worked for.

As it turned out, I had been paying my original call center good money for a good reason, and no other call center could do as well as they did.

"No problem," I thought again. "I got this." So I flipped the script around and created a free trial for the product. Our script was clear and concise: *It's a free trial for just the cost of shipping. You get a three-week supply of the product, and at the end of the three weeks, if you don't cancel your order, we'll automatically ship you a three-month supply at $159.*

Easy enough. My calls per thousand went up, the call center converted well, and I ramped up my advertising to about $50,000 a week. Problem solved.

Within a few months, I got a nasty letter from my merchant provider. They were freezing my account and estimated I would owe about $280,000 in chargebacks. They weren't going to release any of my funds until we filled up a reserve account with that much money to protect themselves and my customers.

The problem now demanded my attention, because the consequences were about to shut us down.

After auditing hundreds of recorded calls from my outsourced call center, it turns out about 60 percent of calls didn't follow my script at all. Instead of "free trial with future paid shipments," they were going off script and telling people it was a free product for the cost of shipping, and that nothing would ever be charged to them again. They were outright lying, and to my target audience of people over fifty, no less. These were rightful disputes. We had some choices to make.

My wife and I stayed up all night talking it through. We could have walked away from the business, or held the call center responsible through litigation. Or we could have chosen to dig our heels in, do the right thing, then work as hard as we could to make sure everyone got their money back.

The next day, I called the merchant provider and negotiated a weekly pre-fund instead of paying the $280,000 all at once. We modified our offer and began monitoring calls more actively. In short, I started doing what I should have done all along: acted like a professional who made sure everything was being done correctly and looking out for the most important people in the process, the customers.

There is no miracle ending for this story. The merchant provider was right, and I paid back over $250,000 in refunds.

That product ran its course on radio, and eventually I took it 100 percent online. This time, I ran it the right way as an e-commerce business for five years and was rewarded well for my efforts. That became the first online business I sold, but it's a cautionary tale. Every misstep could have been avoided.

I chose to step back and let other people do the work that I knew I did well, and the infomercial failed.

I chose to let my ego get in the way of business and let the professional call center go. I undervalued their work the second I thought "I got this." Then I chose to let the business run itself instead of monitoring crucial waypoints, and it got away from me when the next call center didn't follow the script.

At every point where I didn't hold myself and my business to the highest standards, I lost ground, and I paid dearly for it. I *chose* the pain of losing a quarter-million dollars and an awful lot of sleep, because I *didn't choose* the pain of vigilance and care for the thing I had created.

Even if I knew at that time that I wanted to be an EXITpreneur, I couldn't have done it until I was ready to choose the pain of attention to detail, necessary expenses, and responsibility for the structure of the business I was building. We are not only working toward an eventual payday, we are preparing a business that someone else will want to take over and grow once we're done with it.

In the last eight years, I've talked to over five thousand online entrepreneurs. Some of them were just exploring a potential exit, some were ready for one, and some were planning well in advance. They almost always have the vague idea that they're sitting on something valuable, but that's it. Most people I talk to need to do a fair amount of work to catch up on the kind of preparation that an incredible exit requires, and far too many of them refuse to.

Those people might find a Broker or Advisor who will work with them. They might even manage to find a buyer who will bite. But their exit won't be incredible, and they won't be prepared to repeat the process as a successful EXITpreneur. If you're working toward more than just a quick sale at the end of a mediocre run, it's going to take some work. It's going to take some pain. And it's going to pay off in the end.

BOB'S MIRACLE: BETTER LATE THAN NEVER

Bob is exactly the kind of person you'd want to buy a business from. He's genuinely kind, and his motivations for selling were as pure as they could get. In his late thirties, something happened in his life, a miracle of sorts. He never did divulge all of the details, but the end result was a goal to retire at age fifty and join the ministry.

He had run his business alongside a full-time programming job for ten years, and financially he was right on target. His job brought in six figures and his business brought in twice as much with only about ten hours a week of work.

I met Bob a couple of years before he turned fifty, which had been his original target date for his exit. But he was doing well enough and felt like the business was ready, so he sought me out to help him list and sell the business.

For all of his good motivations, clear goals, and likable personality, Bob hadn't run the business like a true professional. He ran everything through credit cards and bank statements, then turned that over to his CPA at the end of the year. With no profit and loss statements and no real financials, this wasn't something a buyer would be excited to take over and grow. It wasn't even something I could give a real valuation opinion on until I got the numbers, so he had some work to do.

I gave Bob recommendations around the documentation he

needed and introduced him to several bookkeepers he could hire, but he chose not to listen. "I've got this," he told me amiably. "I'll just pull in the data from the bank and merchant statements and build it myself."

He went back over the previous three years and, on the surface, did everything a bookkeeper would do, except he did it in Excel. The data was arguably the same as a professional would curate. It looked great. We listed the business, and it went under contract for about $700,000—twice. Each time, the buyers felt like something was off that they couldn't put their finger on.

Because of the way Bob had run the business, their confidence was never quite rock solid. Buyers want to know that they're investing in something safely, and that it's going to be worth growing. When that confidence is shaken, making it through due diligence and to closing is tougher than normal.

I tried to reiterate my recommendations for Bob: "It's intangible, but we're not instilling confidence in buyers. Let's take a couple of weeks and hire a bookkeeper to get the data in QuickBooks and make sure it matches up to what you've done."

This time, he followed through. It cost him $1,500 and a couple of extra weeks. Shockingly—and this is not always the case, by any means—the numbers lined up completely. He had done it all exactly right, so what was the problem?

We decided to troubleshoot by reversing the sale process. We went back to three people on the back-up buyer list and gave them direct access to the due diligence folder before accepting offers. We set out a period of ten days for them to verify the information, ask questions, and then make their best and final offer. On day eleven, if an offer was accepted, we would go directly into the asset purchase agreement drafting and negotiating since due diligence had already been done.

All three buyers agreed, and all three made a best and final offer within ten days. Even though Bob's numbers had been right, not having it structured professionally "didn't feel right" with the first two buyers who we had already gone under Letter of Intent (LOI) with, and those deals fell apart. Now, with everything in QuickBooks, even though the data was exactly the same, Bob got three additional offers and wound up signing an LOI for $50,000 more than the other two offers that had fallen through. And yes—the last LOI made it all the way through to closing.

That additional $50,000 that Bob earned was not a bad ROI for his $1,500 investment. Was it strictly because of QuickBooks data? I cannot say for certain. But time and time again, I see that the more trust and confidence is instilled in buyers, the more risk they are willing to take, and the more money they are willing to pay.

THE NATURE OF RESISTANCE

Business owners are skilled individuals. No matter what kind of product or service you sell, or what platform you build your business on, you've done a lot to get your business off the ground. If you want something done right, you have to do it yourself, right?

Wrong.

Yes, the most important thing is to maintain a business that produces revenue. Along with this, though, you have to properly take care of the financials. Long term, there's no point in producing revenue if it's not tracked well and positioned for someone else to eventually take it over.

As Dave Bryant from EcomCrew often says: "Revenue is vanity and profits are sanity." It's easy to measure revenue without good clean financials. But measuring profit accurately—and more importantly, cash flow and Seller's Discretionary Earnings (SDE) (we'll cover this later)—cannot be done without proper bookkeeping.

Bob was excellent at setting and meeting goals. He was skilled at creating revenue. But he didn't cover all his bases, and it almost cost him his life's goals.

Selling his business became a longer and more emotional process that put his ultimate goal in limbo. Bob chose that pain. By choosing to ignore what needed to be done, he chose to take the long way around. He's fortunate that it was salvageable—he's wise for ultimately making the right decision.

No matter what niche you're in, your expertise doesn't cover every single base on your own. For example, I know that I'm not an expert in developing SaaS businesses. And even though I have a background in content creation, I know that I'm not a great content writer. I know that my PPC experience is dated. And I'm not an expert at developing organic traffic on Google or managing sponsored ads on Amazon, *so I am not going to give you advice on any of that.*

However, I do understand what increases or plummets the value of an online business. I'm great at making sure that both business owners and buyers reach maximum value. I'm great at doing a deep dive into financials and finding details that can sway the true value of your business by tens or hundreds of thousands of dollars. I'm great at spotting the intangibles that can make or break a deal. This hard work upfront isn't done to jack up the list price, but to show the *true earnings* of a business for potential acquirers. Helping entrepreneurs achieve incredible exits is what I do. If it's not what you do, then it's unwise to disregard these recommendations. Odds are, you don't *have this*!

FIGURE OUT WHAT YOU WANT

One thing Bob did really well was set a goal to exit at a certain value, and he focused on that goal nonstop. He knew *why* he was building his business and what he wanted to get out of it. That kind of vision led to his success. He never lost sight of his goals.

By now, you've already begun to see that an incredible exit is possible, so now it's time to bring that possibility into focus. In order to do this, you have to set your goals first. So what's your number? Do you want to sell for $100,000, one million, or ten million? Do you already know what your next adventure will look like and what you'll need to make it happen? Is there something you want to do for or with your family? Think beyond annual revenue and work on a financial and happiness goal for the exit as well.

Don't overthink it at this point—just jot down a number right here in this book. Later on, you can come back and revise it if needed.

I would like to sell my business for _____ dollars in the _____ quarter of the year _____.

Stop reading. Fill out blanks above. Seriously.

Once it is complete, then read on. You will learn that the best way to reverse engineer a path to that goal is to know what your business is worth today. With that knowledge, you can chart a path to your own incredible exit.

That's what you'll learn in this book. You'll learn what brings and plummets value. You'll learn what buyers want and what scares the hell out of them. You'll learn what an add-back is and why it is so critically important to run your business using accrual accounting. You'll learn everything you need to know to understand the value of your business and set an incredible exit goal—and reverse engineer a path to that goal.

If you still have not filled in the blanks, please do. It's a simple but important step to take.

Keep in mind that inventory-based businesses can be sold with a "plus inventory" amount or "including inventory" amount. For simplicity purposes, I'd leave the inventory value out of your goal. Generally speaking you'll get paid your inventory value in addition to that target business value.

I also think it is wise to incorporate how you want to *feel* at closing. It's not all about dollars and zeroes, though those do impact how you feel. There's something more that happens as well. I recently sold a business for someone who became a father two days after his seventeenth birthday, was riddled with debt as an adult, and at some point had dealt with (and overcame) substance abuse. When we recorded his exit interview after selling his online business for multiple seven figures, I asked him how he felt once he knew the deal was done and the business was sold (*not* how he felt about the zeroes in his account). His response was quick and clear: "I felt a huge weight lifted off my shoulders."

He'd been running the business for four years and had battled through cash flow challenges, competition price wars, product innovation, and Amazon algorithm changes that impacted his revenue and risk tolerance often. For him, selling achieved financial peace of mind and the ability to move on to his next adventure knowing himself better, knowing what he didn't want to do, and knowing what type of lifestyle he wanted to live. His next adventure may be helping others overcome some of the challenges he overcame himself.

With this in mind, write down your "feelings" goal as well.

> When I sell my business for _____ dollars, I will feel _____.

You can add as many descriptive words as you see fit. Here are a few examples:

- When I sell my business for $1 million, I will feel a huge burden lifted off my shoulders.
- When I sell my business for $1 million, I will feel a sense of pride!
- When I sell my business for $1 million, I will feel excited for my next adventure that will be ten times bigger!
- When I sell my business for $1 million, I will feel closer to my family as we get to spend more time together.
- When I sell my business for $1 million, I will feel stress-free because I will be out of debt and able to start my next business with plenty of money in the bank.

Once you have a goal in mind, it's time to do some rough math on what kind of sale you'll need in order to meet that goal. Advisor fees and taxes will have to be considered, though there are ways to minimize your tax liability. In any case, how much you sell for is less important than how much you get to keep.

Let's assume you sell for a million in value, excluding any inventory. After a typical fee, you'll end up with about $900,000 in taxable money. Because the sale of a business falls in the realm of capital gains rather than personal income, we can estimate roughly 25 percent in combined state and federal taxes.[2] That takes your million dollars down to a ballpark $675,000 after taxes.

Please keep in mind that the estimated 25 percent changes based on your actual income levels. On the federal side it can currently go as low as 0 and up to 20 percent. On the state side it's all over the place depending on where you live.

Some states have zero state income taxes, so depending on where you live this figure could add an additional 5–13 percent or more.

Unfortunately, some states have incredibly high state income taxes, so that combined 25 percent could go up as well. You know where you live and should know the state income tax percentage. This can have such a negative impact on what's left over after taxes that I've seen people plan their exit a few years in advance so they can move out of high-tax states to save that expense.

The objective with goal-setting here is to determine what you'd like to get out of the sale, then figure out what you'll need to

---

2   There are experts on this subject who can help you create a closer estimate. For resources and referrals, go to EXITpreneur.io.

sell your business for in order to reach both your monetary and happiness goal.

Then it's time to learn as much as you can about what brings or plummets value. Learn everything about the valuation process, how to calculate Seller's Discretionary Earnings (SDE), what buyers want, how deals are structured, etc.—everything you'll learn from this book.

Then you'll make adjustments as needed, and go on to operate your business in such a way that it'll be ready to exit once you get there.

MIKE'S STORY: ADAPTING WHEN NECESSARY

"I knew what to do, and I knew I'd get to it someday. But I woke up, and *someday* was here."

Mike told me this on stage in front of a couple hundred business owners. We were there to create a vision for potential exits, and Mike was just the guy to tell his story. Not because his exit was really perfect, but because it was perfectly real.

In his latest online business, Mike had four separate brands. He had great-looking websites for each and put all four within one seller account on Amazon. He wanted to sell all four brands as one package deal—at least, that was his plan. But, he cautioned the audience, "I didn't think everything through, and some realities caught me off guard." The brands were all commingled, with one tax return and one set of bank accounts and credit cards. He had ten virtual assistants (VAs) all working on all of the brands, and all of the inventory in one place. His dream was to sell it all as one package, because for him it functioned all as one.

The problem is that buyers are looking for the best brands. It's like trading marbles back when some of us were kids—they want to pull the chipped ones out and only get the good ones. When we tried to separate each brand and look at it on its own, there were some chips that had to be repaired.

Later on, we'll talk about What Buyers Want and the four components or pillars of value. Two of Mike's brands didn't fit well with all four pillars. Two of them were very young, and Mike's approach for a new brand was to put a lot of money into ads that got them off the ground. The profit and loss for those two brands showed they were losing money. That, combined with the inherent risk in a very young business, made them undesirable on their own. No matter how ready Mike was to let go of them, they weren't ready to be sold. In fact, they decreased the overall value of his four brands combined.

The two brands that were left were quite attractive. One of them drove more revenue and profit than the other, but its primary stock keeping unit (SKU) came with some intellectual property rights issues. The manufacturer that owned those rights and allowed Mike to sell exclusively online wasn't ready to let those rights transfer to a new owner. In other words, there was a "transferability" issue. Unfortunately, that SKU drove significant revenue and pulling it from the sale hurt the overall value substantially.

Mike is an experienced and savvy entrepreneur, and his eye toward fairness enabled him to work out an arrangement with the manufacturer to plan an exit of that brand twelve to twenty-four months out that would benefit them both. That left us with one final brand.

The final brand made it over the hurdles (through and around the pillars, really) that the other brands had tripped over, so now we just had to make sure the structure would be attractive to buyers. This included new LLCs for each brand, no more commingling of monies or staff, new Amazon Seller Accounts for the brands that were not being sold—and the difficult task of moving inventory out of one seller account to a 3PL (third party logistics), and then back into the new ones. In short, it was a logistical nightmare that occurred during Mike's personal relocation from one state to another. Again, being a typical entrepreneur who's skilled at multitasking, he got it done.

Sure, we could have sold the brand and required the buyer to move it into a new seller account, but that would have increased their risk and workload. In order to get maximum value we chose to do the hard work and make the business more attractive to a broader base of buyers.

As the process moved along, commingling kept rearing its ugly head. First, it prevented the business from being SBA eligible, which narrowed the pool of potential buyers from the outset. And other potential buyers were worried about the way the VAs might transfer. Would Mike keep the best for himself? How did he really track the hours by brand? And so on. What buyers didn't know was that Mike is one of the good guys. He goes above and beyond to help others first—and that includes doing everything he could to improve the value of his business for the buyer's benefit.

When we finally overcame all of the obstacles and found a buyer, that person had a lot on their plate too, and needed an extended closing, which worked out well for both parties.

Mike chose the pain of untangling his businesses before selling one of them at maximum value. He had plans and goals but didn't reverse engineer a path to them with each brand and a buyer in mind.

When Mike woke up ready to sell his business, he was emotionally spent. He wanted out, and had big ideas about what that might mean. Without building toward that plan from the beginning, we couldn't create the full exit that he envisioned. So he had to wake up the next day, still ready to sell, but still obligated to keep going. He had to run the one sellable business for months longer than he wanted to, and still has to run three more for at least another year until they are ready.

With this business Mike waited too long to get things in order to get the full exit of all four brands that he wanted, when he wanted it, but he's an EXITpreneur through and through. He has a plan now. One day he'll have another brand ready to go, and when that time comes, it'll be a breeze. The financials will be clean, it'll be SBA eligible, and there won't be any commingling or questions of trust to overcome.

> **Note:** Being SBA eligible doesn't just mean you'll get more buyers—it means that cash buyers will know there are many more eligible buyers and will likely step up and make an offer faster, at or closer to asking price. Oftentimes, SBA offers do come in slightly higher than cash offers, simply because of the ROI for the buyer when a ten-year note from the SBA is available.

Here's the kicker: While Mike was completely spent and ready to walk away a year ago, knowing that you have a clear plan and a viable end in sight can change your perspective. Mike knows what his objectives are now and what getting the details right can do for the overall process and value at an exit. Now he can enjoy each new milestone and easily jump over each new hurdle along the way. The crazy growth train he's been hanging onto has become thrilling instead of scary, because he's seen where it ends and knows all the stops along the way.[3]

REVERSE ENGINEERING YOUR GOALS

For the sake of argument, let's say you want to sell your business for $2 million. Now what? How are you going to reach that value and achieve your financial goals?

In keeping with our simple numbers, let's say that you can expect a 4x multiple for a business in your category, with your risk factors accounted for. That means you need to reach $500,000 in discretionary earnings in order to reach that $2 million. Not top-line revenue, but complete Seller's Discretionary Earnings (SDE).

If you don't know exactly what that means, don't worry. You're not alone. I'm going to walk you through it, but first things first: please don't even think about saying "I got this" right now. A lot of work and many nuances go into calculating SDE properly. If you set your goals and reverse engineer them using bad data, what's the point? To get the numbers right, you're going to have to do the work. All of it.

So you figure out $2 million is your number, and you determine your SDE is currently $250,000 for the last twelve months. You're going to have to at least double in size in order to reach your target.

---

3   Mike spent a lot of time talking with me about this journey on the *EcomCrew* Podcast. Find our episodes on EXITpreneur.io.

Do not panic.

Remember, we're building toward a goal here, not waiting to see what happens. Great exits aren't lottery tickets. They don't happen by chance. You're going to work for it by running a great business and learning everything you can about what brings value.

It's not simple though, I'm sorry to say. For instance, your $250,000 SDE business may be currently valued at a 3x multiple. But when it grows to $500,000, its value may be 4x because of size, growth trends, age, diversification, and recurring revenues. That's good news, not bad. The details on what brings value will make your focus clear, and we'll get there as the book unfolds.

Aside: If your eyes begin to bleed when this much accounting is talked about in one paragraph...toughen up! Grab a tissue and a beer, whiskey, or a glass of wine, and stick with me. This is *your* business and *your* life's work. And these details will add more value in a few hours than launching your next SKU will—with less risk and more upside. I promise.

Big Aside #2: Keep in mind that businesses with inventory can be listed as a multiple of SDE, OR a multiple of SDE + inventory. There is no clear list price value line that separates those listed one way or the other. But as transaction values climb to the 10–20M +/- range, it is not uncommon for private equity buyers to expect the multiple to be of SDE + inventory.

As you compare firms to list your own business for sale with, keep the above in mind. Those listed with inventory as part of the multiple give the appearance of listing businesses at a higher multiple, when it's not the case.

Example:

Inventory Purchased Separately:

Multiple: 3.5

List Price: $2,275,000 + Inventory (~$600,000)

SDE: $650,000

Inventory Included in the Multiple:

Multiple: 4.42

List Price: $2,875,000 ($2,275,000 in SDE + $600,000 in inventory)

SDE: $650,000

At a glance it would appear the second firm is listing businesses for a higher multiple—and it may attract you as a seller to them. It's not the case though; the value to you at the end of the transaction is the same regardless of the listing multiple (run the math and you'll see).

On the flip side, buyers may glance at the multiples and be more attracted to the first way of listing the business because it appears as though they list businesses at lower multiples that are more attractive to buyers.

Neither way is right or wrong, or intended to trick anyone.

To calculate SDE properly, you're going to look at every single detail in your P&Ls, all the way down to the cash back monies or rewards you get on your business credit card, and make sure you haven't wasted anything. You're going to look at one-time developer expenses, the cost of goods sold (COGS), depreciation, amortization, owner payroll, and payroll taxes. Don't forget about travel to mastermind events and their dues. We'll look at the efficiency of VAs, the bookkeeper who's your cousin and should never have been hired, and the renegotiated COGS you achieved three months ago and how that impacts value. And much, much more.

You're going to get smarter on every single aspect of your business so that you know what you have, where you're going, and how to get there quickly. You're going to work hard for this, and then as soon as it's over you're going to take a well-deserved break and then be ready to do it all again…not only smarter, but also stress- and debt-free.

REALISTIC LIMITS ON YOUR GOALS

What you want out of your business has to include what you *don't* want as well. It's just as important to understand your personal limitations as it is to know what you're driving toward. That moment when you wake up and want out is so often driven by a business that outgrows you, that it's vital to build that moment into your plans. Make sure your goals fall under that threshold, or you won't make it there.

Different people will have different limitations. I once sold a business for a twenty-eight-year-old entrepreneur named Ethan, who knew he was eventually going to go into the family hardware business.

Ethan started an online business in grad school. At twelve

months, we started talking. At twenty-four months, we sold his business for $1 million. Then he and his fiancé traveled around the world for nine months and settled down in Hawaii to get into the family business with a nice financial boost at their backs.

Another owner, Charlie, knew he could take his business to $20 million in revenue and did. He also knew the business was capable of five times that, but that he didn't have the skill-set or the interest to take it that far. He didn't want to deal with the attorneys on retainer, HR, international warehousing, staffing, and the logistics that kind of growth requires. Charlie had different aspirations than Ethan, but he also knew his own limitations and refused to promote himself beyond his own level of competence. So he sought an exit.

A third business owner, Todd, didn't know what his limitations were when he took on investor money. When he had to learn about reporting to his investors and improving his financials, projections, planning, reporting, and communicating, he loved it. He was driven by that kind of energy. It made him better and it made his business better, to the point where it tripled in size three years in a row, and I'm sure it will triple again.

When you factor in your goals and start to make plans down this path—you have to choose the right pain—you need to know the targets you want to sell for. And you need to know where you're at now, and make sure that you have that accurate number. You need to know what motivates you and what's realistic for you to pursue.

Understand, as well, that certain categories within certain niches will have limitations. Some models are less valuable because of channel risks and transferability. If the limits of your niche don't align with your goals and drivers, you're going to struggle to make it all the way there.

That leads me to one final limitation that not everyone agrees with: I believe you should at least *like* the niche or category you are in. You should enjoy providing what you provide, whether it's a product, service, content, or SaaS, because business will get tough. Things will go sideways. When they do—not if, but when—fighting through the tough times will be much easier if you're somewhat passionate about what you do.

If you're already out of your depth, in a category that isn't going to thrive, or stuck with a business you care nothing about, set goals anyway. Know that the end is in sight, even though it's going to be hard to get there.

And yes, I've let some of my own brands "run their course." I've had hard conversations with people who just couldn't make the math work. Sometimes the value of a sale is less than what you'd make after holding it for a few years as it slowly dies on the vine. That's a grind, and it's not an easy choice to make. I can't make it for you, but I can arm you with enough information and tools that you can walk into it with your eyes open, knowing that it's not going to last forever.

WHAT'S THE GAIN FOR ALL THIS PAIN?

Not long ago, after I spoke at an event in Texas, a young man came up and shook my hand. His name was Brandon, and I'd never met him in person before. I had, however, sold his business a couple of years prior! When I sold Brandon's business he was in his early twenties. Over the course of three years, he had found a product he liked, branded it, launched it on Amazon, and then brought it to me to sell for an incredible $600,000 plus the cost of inventory. That payday can be divided up to represent about $200,000 for each of the three years he ran the business, on top of the income he pulled in during that time. Brandon went on to use that money to invest in cryptocurrency, help people with their own online marketing, and then build another brand that he will eventually exit as well. Not bad for a kid just a few years out of high school with no college education.

After another event, this one in Las Vegas, a man came up and shook my hand. I smiled and greeted him, always excited to meet someone new. Then he said, "Joe! It's great to talk to you again." *Whoops.*

Smiling, he continued, "We haven't met in person, but I just wanted to let you know I took the advice you gave me. Since we talked, my son joined the business and things have really turned around. We're having so much fun now. I just wanted to catch you and say thanks."

When people like this get right to work, no matter how far away their exit is, they go on to be happier and more fulfilled in their business. They work just as hard on the exit as any other stage of growth, because they know it all goes together. They understand just how much of their money is going to come from the exit, so the details are more exciting than painful. The details are markers on the way to the goal, which will ultimately fund the next set of goals.

Let's go back to that $1 million sale one more time (or 10x the numbers if that suits and/or motivates you). Now you've got about $775,000 in cash (this includes $100,000 of inventory you got paid for). Think about how little you had to work with when you bootstrapped your first business, and how much $775,000 could change that scenario. You could put some away for retirement, pay off debt, draw on some of it for your lifestyle over the next couple of years, and still take out $50,000 to start your next venture.

Not only are you starting out with more cash after that first exit, but now you know exactly what pitfalls to avoid as you build toward the next. You won't commingle or forget to outsource bookkeeping. You'll have your expertise around product launches and ranking and profitability. You'll know how to work SEO or network with SaaS developers. The unexpected will always take its toll, but not like it did in the beginning. Not like it does when you don't have a plan, knowledge, and firsthand experience.

Strangely, far too many *still* prefer the ego of top-line numbers to the nitty-gritty work of building a brand they can exit someday. These are the people who can't see the forest of an exit for the trees of everyday income and expenses. They're stuck on a treadmill, running for their lives, without an end in sight. Sadly, for that pain, there is little to be gained.

If you're still not sure whether you'll ever sell, it can't hurt to at least keep reading. And if you know it's time to sell, it'll hurt a whole lot more if you don't. Either way, it's time to dig into the details. It's time to learn what kind of value you're sitting on, and how you can make the most of it.

PART II

THE VALUATION SCOREBOARD

CHAPTER 3

VALUATION OVERVIEW

The first and most common question I hear from business owners is, "What kind of multiple are things selling for now?" They've heard someone in a mastermind group or on a forum or in their peer group talk about their multiple, they have a vague idea of what their business is worth, and they think the multiple is the missing piece—the magical factor that will reveal their true value.

Be honest: you've thought the same thing, haven't you? It's okay. You're in good company. I'm not even going to touch your multiple for a while though. It simply doesn't matter until some other key details are sorted out.

After hearing that question thousands of times and knowing it's not even close to the information they need to know at that stage, I've learned to ask a question in return: "Multiple of *what*?"

A multiple is applied to the Seller's Discretionary Earnings (SDE), which is net income plus add-backs over a period of twelve months. Simple enough—until you start to question what add-backs are, or if the data in your profit and loss (P&L) is using the correct accounting method. Anywhere from 10 to 30 percent of discretionary earnings can come from add-backs, and not everyone digs deep enough to find them all. An inexperienced Broker or a direct sale to a buyer might give you a 3x multiple or even more, but if it's based off a low or incorrect discretionary earnings calculation, your total valuation could be extremely low and flat-out wrong. Or, sometimes worse, it could be listed too high and then the deal will get renegotiated or fall apart in due diligence.

YOU PUT DOLLARS IN THE BANK (NOT MULTIPLES)

Several years ago, a client (husband and wife) from New Zealand came to me with a drop-ship wig business and an art supply business. We had spoken for some time about the first, but the second had taken off like a rocket and they were excited and eager to sell. They were so excited to sell that they had gone under contract to buy a house, contingent upon the sale of the business.

For four years, they had enjoyed the flexibility of running an e-commerce business by traveling while they worked and raising their little girl. But it was time to settle down, and their atypical (foreign) income made it difficult to secure a bank loan. The only way to establish the roots they were hoping for would be to buy the house for cash, and that cash was wrapped up in the sale of their business.

"Full disclosure, Joe," they told me. "We've spoken to two other brokerage firms as well, and they've given us a multiple. We want to run it by you, too, since we already have a relationship."

I started the valuation process, as usual, by digging into their financials to figure out what they actually had. About 80 percent of their revenue came from Amazon and 20 percent from a separate e-commerce platform, which effectively made it an Amazon business, and after just eighteen months, it was very young. Combine all of that with a couple of hero SKUs and there was a good bit of risk to overcome.

A "hero SKU" is when one SKU drives the majority of the revenues.

In spite of the obvious risk factors, the other firms had edged the multiple up to 3.2 and 3.3 in order to reach the seller's financial goals. In my experience, trying to artificially inflate a value with a stretched multiple doesn't work. Instead of following suit or sending them away, I looked closely at the financials they'd provided to see what else we might be able to use. It didn't take long to have our answer.

One of the first things I found was that their financials were presented using cash-basis accounting. That means they entered their expenses in QuickBooks within the month the expense occurred. But for a bootstrapped e-commerce or Amazon business that's growing rapidly, you're constantly buying inventory to keep up with sales. In this situation, using cash-basis accounting depresses your SDE and the overall value of your business.

Instead, we worked out how to calculate their landed cost of goods sold on an accrual basis, which is the Generally Accepted Accounting Principles (GAAP) method, then shifted the P&L accordingly. This one change to the correct accounting method more accurately demonstrated their income—and increased their SDE by about $75,000. That allowed us to bring the multiple down to a more reasonable 2.7 in light of the business risks and actually *exceed* their financial goals. Their business sold at full asking price for all cash, and it closed within thirty days.

They bought their dream home, and I now have two new friends in New Zealand.

There are enough layers between your business and its multiple that you could lose tens of thousands of dollars—and potentially the realization of your goals—if you get the details wrong. A too-high multiple will make buyers skeptical and may even prevent them from looking at your listing. A too-low calculation of financials will leave money on the table.

You've worked hard for years risking everything for your business. When you sell it is no time to rush. You've got to get all of the details right, and present a great business for sale to attract a great buyer—and at a great price for both parties. Do this right, and you might get multiple offers and get to choose your buyer. In these chapters, we're going to demystify the layers of this process so that the eventual multiple makes sense and facilitates an accurate value for everyone involved.

I won't make up anything new or kitschy or unique to get my point across. I won't create a language only you and I understand. We're just going to clear up already existing technical terms and data points that are muddy for almost every first-time (and second-time) seller. We're going to pull the veil back so that you get it right this time and are ready to do it right from the get-go next time.

Your EXITpreneur journey really does start here: with a clear understanding of what the valuation of a business entails.

BUSINESS VALUATION FORMULA

Net Income

+ Add-Backs

= Seller's Discretionary Earnings (SDE)

SDE

x

Multiple

= List Price of the Business

If your business holds inventory, you'd also add "plus the landed cost of good, sellable inventory on hand at the time of closing" for most transactions.

Alternatively, you might see some listings that include the value of inventory in the list price. This makes the multiples look higher, but the end result or total value is the same.

At some point a SaaS business may sell for a multiple of revenue instead of earnings. This is covered later on in the book.

NET INCOME: PROPER ACCOUNTING COMES FIRST

The skillset required to grow a business with millions of dollars in revenue is not the same skillset required to keep track of those financials accurately. It's an unfortunate truth. Most of us who wind up as business owners didn't start off as book-keepers, and it was by choice. We didn't want to pay attention to it or we didn't know how to, yet we became entrepreneurs. And suddenly, bookkeeping and accounting can't be ignored. What now?

For as many hats as a business owner has to wear, in my opinion, accounting should not be one of them. It's not something to slog through yourself, or to outsource to your brother, sister, aunt, uncle, spouse, or neighbor. Your financials should be tracked by a professional e-commerce bookkeeper using proper accounting methods. The cost is not excessive—usually $100 to $2000 per month, depending on the size and complexity of the business. In exchange, you get to free up the time you would've spent chasing the numbers, likely while inputting them inaccurately. You'll also gain a whole lot of peace of mind and value when you eventually exit your business. The correct P&Ls, balance sheets, cash flow statements, etc., are easy to run or show up in your inbox every month, and they're ready for you when it's time to assess your progress toward your exit goals.

With that said, there is a lot of confusion around hiring an accountant or bookkeeper to manage your financials.

Here's my view:

A bookkeeper (not a CPA) should be hired to enter the data into QuickBooks Online (QBO) or Xero every month. The best ones do it with great accuracy and proper accounting, making it easy for your CPA to review your P&Ls and help you plan any tax mitigation strategies and file your taxes. These bookkeepers will even help you with cash flow planning and a variety of other essential financial-oriented items that will help you run your business more professionally and with less stress.

Lots of entrepreneurs mistakenly hire CPAs to do their bookkeeping, and when I see the P&Ls and the vast amount of adjustments, it's much more complex to firm up the accurate value of the business.

Many CPAs will make annual lump sum adjustments on inventory values, instead of setting QBO or Xero up properly to do monthly accrual accounting. Accurate monthly figures are essential and lump sum annual adjustments throw things off and make the P&L look "lumpy." Bookkeepers are trained on accounting software like Xero and QBO and know them inside out. CPAs are trained on tax laws and help with tax mitigation. They are generally not experts on accounting software, which is needed to accurately reflect your financial situation month in and month out.

But hiring the right bookkeeper isn't all there is to it. You want someone who is familiar with your platform and, especially if you're in e-commerce, who will specifically run your numbers on an accrual instead of on a cash basis. My clients in New Zealand made the mistake of doing it themselves and used cash-basis accounting, and it almost cost them their dream home. Few people understand this crucial distinction.

Let's say you bought a thousand units of a product in August, at a cost of $10 per unit—a total of $10,000, with 30 percent down. After that $3,000 expense, the products spent eight weeks in production and four weeks on the boat from China. By the first of October, you own the other $7,000, but the product won't be in circulation until Black Friday and the holiday season.

In cash-basis accounting, that would show up in your P&L as $10,000 of expenses that's only partially reflected in income. The $3,000 would show up in August, and the $7,000 would show up in October before the product left the port in China.

The new year will roll over before all of the thousand pieces have sold. If you calculate your Seller's Discretionary Earnings from there, you'll have $10,000 worth of expenses that haven't fully produced an income. Not only does this hurt your SDE, but it's not an accurate picture of the health of your business.

Accrual accounting puts that expense on the balance sheet, and it only goes onto the P&L once one of the units has sold.

Revisiting our initial example, let's say the products land in November. Every time one of the units sells, its cost goes into your accounting system. If all of the thousand units sold in the month of December, then the entire expense would show up then too. Not just the top-line cost, but whatever it costs per unit for it to land at your fulfillment center. With the "landed" cost of goods sold tracked as the goods are actually sold, the P&L reflects your expenses as they relate to your income. It's the only way to accurately gauge discretionary earnings, especially for product-based e-commerce businesses.

A TALE OF TWO P&LS

Below are two abbreviated P&Ls for the same business, one using cash-based accounting, the other accrual-based. This business is a rapidly growing, product-oriented business that requires heavy cash outlay to keep up with increasing inventory demand.

Note the huge fluctuations in the landed COGS percentage in the first P&L and its impact on the bottom line. This is the first thing I look at for product-based businesses. I calculate the COGS as a percentage of total income to determine if the business owner is using cash- or accrual-based accounting.

In the cash P&L, the total COGS is 36 percent. In this example, the *real* COGS is just 31 percent. Note what this does to the bottom line in the accrual-based P&L.

Chapter 3: A Tale of Two PLs

Accrual-Based P&L

	Jan	Feb	Mar	Apr	May	Jun	Jul	Aug	Sep	Oct	Nov	Dec	Total
Total Revenue	78,623	82,687	91,006	100,326	121,698	117,331	172,564	156,983	169,354	186,231	211,562	236,005	1,724,370
Cost of Sales													
Total Cost of Goods Sold	24,373	25,633	28,212	31,101	37,726	36,373	53,495	48,665	52,500	57,732	65,584	73,162	534,555
COGS % of Revenue	31%	31%	31%	31%	31%	31%	31%	31%	31%	31%	31%	31%	31%*
Gross Profit	54,250	57,054	62,794	69,225	83,972	80,958	119,069	108,318	116,854	128,499	145,978	162,843	1,189,815
Other Expenses	38,525	40,517	44,593	49,160	59,632	57,492	84,556	76,922	82,983	91,253	103,665	115,642	844,941
Net Income	15,725	16,537	18,201	20,065	24,340	23,466	34,513	31,397	33,871	37,246	42,312	47,201	344,874
Total Add Backs	1,621	1,581	1,123	1,893	1,842	1,569	1,889	1,363	1,691	986	1,594	1,932	19,084
Total SDE	17,346	18,118	19,324	21,958	26,182	25,035	36,402	32,760	35,562	38,232	43,906	49,133	363,958†

*A steady % means accrual accounting. †This is $92,429 higher than the cash P&L, and it is right.

Cash-Based P&L

	Jan	Feb	Mar	Apr	May	Jun	Jul	Aug	Sep	Oct	Nov	Dec	Total
Total Revenue	78,623	82,687	91,006	100,326	121,698	117,331	172,564	156,983	169,354	186,231	211,562	236,005	1,724,370
Cost of Sales													
Total Cost of Goods Sold	22,801	25,633	29,122	36,117	75,453	62,185	31,062	83,201	113,467	63,319	84,625	0	626,984
COGS % of Revenue	29%	31%	32%	36%	62%	53%	18%*	53%	67%	34%	40%*	0%*	36%
Gross Profit	55,822	57,054	61,884	64,209	46,245	55,146	141,502	73,782	55,887	122,912	126,937	236,005	1,097,386
Other Expenses	38,525	40,517	44,593	49,160	59,632	57,492	84,556	76,922	82,983	91,253	103,665	115,642	844,941
Net Income	17,297	16,537	17,291	15,049	-13,387	-2,347	56,946	-3,140	-27,097	31,659	23,272	120,363	252,445
Total Add Backs	1,621	1,581	1,123	1,893	1,842	1,569	1,889	1,363	1,691	986	1,594	1,932	19,084
Total SDE	18,918	18,118	18,414	16,942	-11,545	-778	58,835	-1,777	-25,406	32,645	24,866	122,295	271,529

*High fluctuations indicate cash accounting. †5% over inflated.

With the accrual P&L there is a gain of $92,429 in SDE. Apply that times a multiple of, say, 3.2 and you've changed the list price by $295,772.80. I'd say the *pain* of flipping your accounting from cash to accrual is worth it. Wouldn't you?

Now let's look at those same factors for a content site. Let's say you're writing about your passion for gluten-free cooking, and you start to gain organic traffic as people enjoy reading about your knowledge and experience. Each week, you're updating information, and more people are reading and subscribing. Eventually you gain a reputation. More traffic, more subscribers, and more readership and trust earn you more authority, and soon you're considered a solid resource for reliable information.

With that authority comes monetization.

You might start simple with a Google AdSense widget that will have ads pop up in a certain part of every page. The ads will be related to your topic or to something the reader has already been looking at, so when they read your article about a new ingredient, and that ingredient is advertised, they might click it. Google or Tribal Fusion—or another ad source—will pay you for each click. Or you might start to use affiliate links, where you would link directly to that ingredient on Amazon. When they click through and purchase the ingredient, you get a percentage of the revenue.

Another way to monetize might be to review products. You might review cookbooks or cutting boards or restaurants in your part of the world, sharing your expert opinion about them and collecting a payout when someone buys products or gift cards from them.

In each of these scenarios, the content creation, traffic growth, and clicks or purchases happen forty-five to sixty days *before* the payout itself.

The revenue that you produce in the month of August doesn't pay out until sometime in October. The faster you're growing, the more dramatic the lag. If you decide to sell your gluten-free site in the month of August, cash-basis numbers won't reflect the true picture of your growth. If you're growing by 10 or 15 percent month over month, you'll lose all of that in your earnings line, and your overall business value, based on the numbers, will be less than its true value.

Tracking actual revenue in hand is easier on a cash basis, but it will almost always leave some value on the table at an exit if the business is in growth mode. For some clients, it can be a significant amount lost. I had one client whose content business was growing by $10,000 in profit per month. On a cash basis, that's $10,000 lost for every month we were behind. Her business was paid about 60 days out—so $20,000 in increased profit times a multiple of, say, 4 leaves $80,000 on the table at an exit. Good for the buyer, bad for the inexperienced EXITpreneur.

If you are a buyer and someone is listing their business on their own, you could find yourself in an instant equity position. If the seller has not read this book and is using cash accounting for a rapidly growing business, they are likely undervaluing their business because they miscalculated their SDE. Sadly, this happens all too often and I call it "the ignorance discount."

Accrual-based accounting is a little trickier, but it shows those earnings even if you haven't been paid for them yet. And if you're outsourcing the bookkeeping tasks to an expert, you'll gain value and peace of mind. And the cost will more than pay for itself.

> ## HIRE A BOOKKEEPER
>
> Remember our friend Bob in Chapter 2? Even though his numbers were exactly right, buyers wouldn't bite unless a professional had been the one to prepare them. I want you to understand this for your sake, but don't mistake this for a DIY manual. My advice is for you to hire an e-commerce bookkeeper. You can find a list of them in the resource section of EXITpreneur.io.

ADD-BACKS: A COMPLETE PICTURE OF THE BUSINESS

Remember that:

SDE = Net Income + Add-Backs

Even if the bookkeeping is done correctly, your add-back calculations still need to be done separately by your Advisor (not bookkeeper) and are critical.

Add-backs are confusing and often misunderstood. Many of them are the perks you get from the business, but they go way beyond simple owner benefits. Add-backs are how we factor in the owner benefits that are not seen on the net income line alone. Because it's such a complex process, even some Advisors, Brokers, and Investment Bankers get this wrong. You can only maximize add-backs if you're looking hard for them, in all possible areas.

If you're calculating your discretionary earnings with only your payroll added back, you could be leaving a lot on the table. There's still your car, meals, personal development, cash back points that slide over to your personal account, and reward points that you've never cashed in. Anything that's an owner benefit, sometimes obvious and sometimes not, should factor into your SDE via the add-back schedule.

When add-backs are left out of the SDE, it's not just that amount that's lost. It's that amount times your multiple. If you are off by $5,000 and your business is listed at a 3x multiple, you are undervaluing it by $15,000. These are real dollars you've worked very hard to earn. Rushing to list your business because accounting makes your eyes bleed is just going to cost you money. It's worth getting right not just for your value on the table, but for the buyers to have a complete picture of the business.

In Chapters 10 and 11, we'll look closer at the Financial Key Metrics to track and take a deep dive into the Three Levels of Add-Backs. When tracking these things becomes second nature for you, selling gets that much easier.

Here's a teaser of what an Add-Back Schedule might look like below your net income line.

Chapter 3: PL with Add-Back Schedule

Total Net Income	6,190	5,379	16,228	4,487	11,280	-856	11,611	28,695	21,799	28,770	53,184	110,975	297,742
Add Backs													
Owner Payroll	4,095	4,095	4,095	4,095	4,095	4,095	4,095	4,095	4,095	4,095	4,095	4,095	49,143
Health Insurance (Owner)	493	493	493	493	493	493	493	493	493	493	493	493	5,916
Amortization	0	0	0	2,137	0	0	0	0	0	0	0	0	2,137
Depreciation	0	0	0	0	0	0	0	0	0	0	0	326	326
Charitable Contributions	0	0	0	300	0	0	0	300	0	0	0	300	900
Interest Expense	317	326	362	301	299	276	272	259	248	201	189	156	3,206
Owner Payroll Taxes (not income)	311	311	311	311	311	311	311	311	311	311	311	311	3,730
Office Supplies (laptop)	0	0	0	0	0	2,300	0	0	0	0	0	0	2,300
Total Travel (Personal)	56	19	1,632	213	22	0	0	79	82	0	1,231	561	3,895
Mastermind Fees	117	117	117	117	117	117	117	117	117	117	117	117	1,404
Cash-Back Money	697	721	881	880	1,295	1,459	922	889	994	1,012	1,142	1,196	12,088
COGS reduction in TTM	1,739	3,868	1,901	1,994	1,764	4,167	6,563	2,009	1,337	0	0	0	25,342
Total Add Backs	7,825	9,950	9,792	10,841	8,396	13,218	12,773	8,552	7,677	6,229	7,578	7,555	110,387
Total SDE	14,015	15,329	26,020	15,328	19,676	12,362	24,384	37,247	29,477	34,999	60,762	118,530	408,130

TRAILING TWELVE MONTHS

I know this is a book, and it is easy to flip back a few pages—but let me repeat it here so the formula becomes ingrained in your memory:

Net Income

+ Add-Backs

= Seller's Discretionary Earnings (SDE)

The vast majority of the time, an online business is valued as a multiple of the trailing twelve month's SDE. If we averaged two or three years instead, the trends of the business could do a disservice for you or the buyer, depending on the trajectory. If we just did the past six months, seasonality might affect it. The only way for the buyer to properly calculate their return on investment (ROI) is to base it off of the past—or *trailing*—twelve months, starting from your listing date or with a short pro forma to include the few months it may take to close from that list date.

BUT WAIT, THERE'S MORE!

It can be seen as a badge of honor for a business owner to have a high multiple. But if the valuation isn't based on accurate numbers—if the earnings weren't calculated properly or the multiple doesn't reflect the true value of the business—you're either going to lose money or stay a business owner instead of being able to exit.

As we dig into the process of a valuation together, almost every step is about the buyer and what they need to know to feel confident in your business so that you can hand it off to them and move on to your next adventure.

We calculate the investment and its potential return *for the buyer*. We ask what the *buyer* is getting, and what it's worth. Artificially high numbers don't help anyone.

If simple definitions were enough to answer those questions, I wouldn't be writing a book. At this point you should have a better idea of what factors a business valuation is based on, but you're probably not ready to dive in and crunch the numbers just yet. In fact, I bet you have a lot of questions right now, and might be flipping through the chapters to find the answers. That's fine.

For now, you might be able to run a quick P&L, check your accounting method, maybe start to see the shape your financials are in—but that's it. Don't bother trying to get your add-backs together or to think about risk and multiples yet. It's not time.

What you can start thinking about—the reason that we do this work to such detail—is that it's not about you at all. Think about the person who will buy your business and what they will want to know, whether you sell a physical product or have a SaaS business or a content site. Think about how important it will be for them to have good data and a complete picture of the business.

The formula for business valuations is just the tip of the iceberg. This goes much deeper than a multiple of the SDE. SaaS buyers want to know about churn rates and monthly and annual recurring revenue. Content buyers want to know about keyword rankings and writers and transferability. Physical product business buyers will want to know about your reviews and competition and defensibility.

In other words, what I've told you so far is just enough to be dangerous.

I've given you an idea of the structure. Think about having an orange belt in karate. You've moved through a couple of ranks and feel like you're getting tough, until someone half your size and twice your age shows up with a brown belt and throws you to the ground without breaking a sweat.

That, more or less, is what we've covered so far. Don't go picking fights with your business's future just yet. Keep reading and learning, because there's a whole lot of technique still to go.

TIME OUT

Head over to QuickBooks or Xero and run a profit and loss statement with a "monthly view" for the last 24 months (if possible). Check the "accrual method" box. Then export it to Excel. Now take your monthly cost of goods sold by month, and divide it by your revenue by month. If it's roughly the same every month, congratulations. You're running on an accrual accounting method. If you're seeing 20 percent, 80 percent, and then 0 percent, you've got some work to do to flip it over to accrual. Hire a bookkeeper who knows how to do it. For a list of highly qualified bookkeepers, head over to EXITpreneur.io and visit our resource page.

And if you can't just pop into an accounting software to get your numbers, this task is even more urgent. Hire that bookkeeper now.

CHAPTER 4

WHAT BUYERS WANT (AND FEAR)

As the business owner, you just want to know what your business is worth and if it can be sold. After all, your life is about to change for the better. You're going to get a fat check, get free of your business, and get on to the next thing. The buyer, on the other hand, is making what may be the biggest purchase of their life. They're going to scrutinize every last detail, and for good reason.

Therefore, the purchase price is never a simple multiple of the Seller's Discretionary Earnings.

Real-life variables sway the value of the business in either direction, and after more than a decade in this business, I've clearly seen that buyers have consistently focused on four categories: risk, growth, transferability, and documentation. These are the Four Pillars of Value that will either be a boost for your business or will make buyers think twice.

Remember, your buyer is ultimately the person who determines what your business is worth. It doesn't matter how good your earnings or multiple looks on paper. If they're uncomfortable with a component of one of these four pillars and you don't have a good answer to back it up or a solution to account for it, the whole structure could topple.

> Note: The Four Pillars of Value is a framework that was developed at Quiet Light over more than a decade using input from thousands of buyers. These pillars are the most important non-mathematical factors when determining a business's value. Overlook these and you are racing toward a finish line with no reward and no end.

IGNORANCE IS NOT BLISS

Every time I have an initial consultation call with a curious entrepreneur, I cover each of these four pillars alongside their discretionary earnings. What we learn about the business's strengths and weaknesses with these pillars tells us what our path forward needs to look like in order to make the business valuable to a buyer. Sometimes we find weaknesses that can be firmed up and turned into strengths. Sometimes we can't fix what's not ideal, but we can make a plan to offset it. Sometimes we find dealbreakers.

When Mike, whose entrepreneurial journey was shared in Chapter 2, wanted to sell all four of his brands as a package deal, we evaluated each of them against these four pillars—Risk, Growth, Transferability, and Documentation—and found that three of the brands were weak enough to jeopardize the entire deal. Of those three, one brand failed completely when the main SKU couldn't be sold online by anyone but Mike. It had a Transferability Pillar issue. Two other brands failed the Risk Pillar. They were too young and, in fact, were losing money in the early stages. They brought down the overall value of the packaged business.

The earlier you can do a thorough valuation that spots those weaknesses, the stronger you'll be when it's time to sell. More importantly, you'll have more emotional strength to keep building each pillar up until the business is *ready* to be sold.

My friend and colleague Chuck Mullins likes to say, "You have to get ugly fast," and it's true. We can't shy away from the reality of our businesses here, so let's get ugly fast and identify the warts and let people see them for what they are. Only then can we work toward fixing issues and highlighting the positive attributes.

If you can't get ugly fast, or if you choose to keep your head down to just focus on driving revenue and barely keeping up with cash flow, you're not really steering this ship. It's going to carry you off in who-knows-what direction, and when you want to get off, you won't know where the hell you are (or what your business is really worth). It's up to you to get your bearings.

And honestly? That's the last thing you want to do when you're emotionally toast and just want to get off the damn ship altogether.

It's not fun preparing and planning, but it's less fun getting stuck in a business you want out of. Learn the valuation process as soon as you can, and outsource the miserable tasks that need to be done. Pay someone else to do it. It's cheap. It's worth every penny. Face the mess now and clean it up for your buyer.

And hey, if you're feeling wiped out and are tired of finding weak spots, it's going to be okay. That just means you've found goals to work toward, and the only thing an EXITpreneur loves more than a goal is a "sold" business. We're shooting for both, and these pillars will have you well on your way.

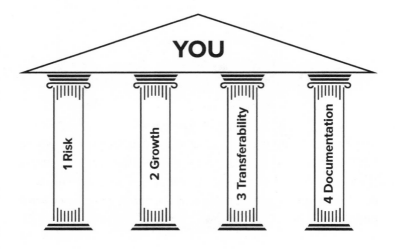

CHAPTER 5

RISK

Remember, the Four Pillars of Value were developed over more than a decade. Don't take them lightly just because it's not math. These were developed through constant feedback from buyers… the ones who wire the funds and write the checks for your businesses!

As much as business owners want Advisors to give them good news, we don't decide anything. This is all about the buyer. Our job is to identify what's going to attract buyers or scare them away, and there's nothing scarier than risk.

Buyers have proven over and over again that if there's too much risk, they'll not offer as much for the business, or they'll pass altogether. Of course, everything we do in life carries risk, so we have to get more specific than that.

SIX KEY FACTORS FOR THE RISK PILLAR

1. Size and Age

2. Defensibility

3. Dependencies

4. Channel

5. Competition

6. Obsolescence

SIZE AND AGE

This pillar starts with the foundation of the size and age of the business. It's not advisable to put a three-month-old business up for sale. You just won't get much money for it. As a rule of thumb, buyers like the twenty-four-month mark, at a minimum. There's still some age and some stability, but there should be a lot of growth as well.

There are exceptions to every rule, and businesses younger than twenty-four months old are sellable. They are just worth less because of the risk associated with the young age of a business.

First-time buyers are only willing to risk so much, so they often like to start out with a younger, smaller business, thinking it is safer. In reality, smaller businesses can be a much higher risk even if the dollar value is lower. It could be a site that depends entirely on SEO or on one super affiliate. It could be a 100 percent Fulfillment by Amazon (FBA) business with a hero SKU. Or it could have just one source of traffic or revenue. Whatever the channel, if there's only one of them, it's going to increase your risk.

> Remember: A hero SKU is one that represents the majority of revenues for a business. Without strong IP, this represents a huge risk to a business. And the more risk there is, the lower the value.

As a business ages, you're no longer drinking through the fire hose of traffic, cash flow, inventory, developers, and content writers. Life starts to get a little easier. You start to earn more and work less. Your systems are in place, and your traffic comes from more stable, varied sources. Just when that peak is reached, you're in the sweet spot. You don't have the risk of early volatility or late-stage antiquation.

The key for older businesses is to age well.

Last year, I sold an eight-year-old SaaS business that had blossomed out of the owner's need to solve a problem. He was a developer who did solve the problem but didn't keep up with the times. Other companies that started three years later used better code and a user-friendly front-facing site, and these competitors grew ten times bigger. If you have custom code, content on a Dreamweaver site, or a complex e-commerce platform, the buyer is going to have to work to update them. In the process of bringing the business into modern times, they might also lose their organic rankings or trigger some other catastrophic crash. That's a risk you're asking the buyer to take on, and they'll drop the value of the business for it.

DEFENSIBILITY

Picture two businesses that are equal in size. One gets 90 percent of their revenue from a single hero SKU that can be found on Alibaba after sixty seconds of searching. The other has a utility patent with thousands of reviews at four and a half stars. Guess which one a buyer will feel confident in?

That's defensibility.

A SaaS business with high recurring revenue on a monthly basis, or a content business with lots of organic traffic and thousands of long-tail keywords, will be defensible. Someone won't be able to set up shop overnight and start competing against you.

The more defensible the business, the lower the risk. Buyers will be willing to pay a higher multiple and spend more money when you've built something that will stand on its own two feet.

DEPENDENCIES

Some businesses are completely dependent on their founder. I couldn't buy Martha Stewart's brand and expect to just replace her. I'm not Martha Stewart and never will be—if she goes away, then at least some of the business goes away. For the most part, the brand is entirely dependent on her. When launching a business, you have to think about whether you're becoming your own version of Martha Stewart.

A few years ago, I helped a woman sell her prepper website. If you aren't familiar, a prepper website is for people who believe a catastrophe of massive proportion is coming soon, and that we should be prepared for the dramatic changes that will come with the apocalypse. She wrote about her experiences as a prepper on a blog, where she recommended products and earned affiliate money for those recommendations. When she reached out to me, she was ready to sell and move on. But because the customers trusted *her* and *her* opinion, the business was dependent on her. To buy that website and suddenly have another person behind the content would be risky—the customers may go away once the person they've grown to depend on disappears.

If you're the name and face of your business, you need to think carefully about the future and how you might be able to transition that branding to a new owner. If you're just starting out, find a way to present it without your name and face at the forefront if at all possible. It's going to be harder to sell if you're the only person talking, even if it's your expertise and passion behind the scenes. It'll still be sellable—it's just going to be harder and will come with more risk to the buyers. For the prepper site, she stayed on board as the spokesperson for twelve months after closing as they transitioned to a new expert and voice. She was able to sell the business, but her next adventure was slightly delayed.

Other dependencies include customer or SKU concentration. Say you have a SaaS business with 500 customers who renew on a monthly basis, but 250 of them come from a single corporation that subscribes for all of their employees. You don't really have 500 customers—you have 251. If that one corporation decided not to renew, half of your revenue would be gone in an instant.

The same goes for SKUs. If 70 percent of your revenue is on one hero SKU, competitors can swoop in, undercut you, and take your business. This scares buyers, which will make them pay less.

CHANNEL

Size and age gave us a window into the channel risks we need to be cautious of. The more channels of revenue we have, the less risk we carry. A business that's 95 percent dependent on Amazon carries a greater risk than one that's half Amazon and half Shopify. Balanced channels are simply worth more, because you're less likely to lose it all if one goes sour.

To clarify, channels don't refer *only* to Amazon, eBay, Target, Shopify, WooCommerce, Etsy, or Wayfair, etc. Those *are* channels, but ultimately we're looking at sources of traffic and revenue. For example, consider a service business that made about $80,000 a month in recurring revenue, but $40,000 of it was from one particular client. That's a risky channel.

When you own your own website and you create the traffic, it is still a single channel, but you own the customer and "channel risk" is hardly an issue at all for most buyers. On a third-party platform like Amazon or eBay, you can't just send your customers texts or connect with them on Facebook. You can't reach out for a second, third, or fourth order, or a new update to your service or SKU. This puts the control in a third party's hands, creating channel risk that your buyer will absolutely consider. And while diversifying to Amazon in Canada, Europe, and Australia is truly diversification, it's still an FBA business that comes with more risk than your own URL where you own the customers.

COMPETITION

Competition risk stems from similar fears. How hard is it to compete with you, and what are the barriers that keep others from doing so?

Are you a drop-ship business that doesn't cost a lot to get into, where everyone already sells what you sell? Are you selling a low-cost SKU that invites people to jump in at any given moment to compete? Has competition made your margins tighter? Do you have the ability to fend off the competitors that do show up?

Once competitors start driving prices down, business gets tough. Some are able to rise above by doing a better job at everything—photos, customer service, reviews, updates with software, better content, a better-looking website, etc. But that's a lot of work, and a buyer who suspects they'll have to claw their way through the market will not hold your business at a high value.

OBSOLESCENCE

Competition and channels aren't the only things that can pull the rug out from under a business. Complete obsolescence is a fear as well. In the electronic space especially, things are always changing and evolving. Buyers become concerned about widgets that might not last the year—cables, phone chargers, adapters, and such—because it's a tough space to be in. In any niche, if buyers fear you'll become obsolete in the near future, you won't get the same value as a business that's perceived to be evergreen.

If you do have an electronics business or any niche that comes with a fear of obsolescence, it's your job to help buyers overcome that fear. If you can't, they won't make offers—or at least not offers that you like.

Don't bury your head in the sand. Come up with the next evolution of your product now—and get it ready for your buyer to take over and continue to grow. Reduce their risk and get rewarded.

You're in it every day, so you might not believe it's really a threat, but those from the outside looking in will not feel as confident as you. I GUARANTEE IT. So what steps can you take to have buyers see what you see? Is it a matter of increasing your customer base? Should you give them something new that de-risks the business to bolt onto that product or service that may eventually go away? Should you diversify?

Sometimes a business has to work on all six of these components of the overall Risk Pillar in order to make their business sellable. The more you can look at your business from the outside and a buyer's point of view, the more you'll be able to fix the weaknesses and focus on the strengths. When buyers see you as a less risky investment, they'll pay higher multiples or higher values.

TIME OUT

- Is your business well-aged, or will it be when it's time to sell? Think...two years as a minimum for a fair valuation, three to four years to instill more confidence in buyers.

- Do you have any IP, exclusive contracts, strong SEO, a huge customer base with recurring revenues, or a massive review or customer count compared to your competitors? Get defensive and your value will rise.

- Do you have a hero SKU producing 50 percent or more of your revenues? Just one manufacturer with no back-ups? Are you the brand and why people buy your product or service? How about one client that represents 60 percent of your revenue? Watch out for lots of dependencies—too many will reduce value.

- Are you a single-channel business? An FBA business is more risk than when you own the customer. A SaaS business with 100 users is great, but not when seventy-two are from one company. Should you expand channels or focus on what you are best at with an exit value in mind? Set goals and know what drives you. What really sets you apart from the competition? "Better customer service" as a differentiator is not going to excite your buyers. Do better.

- Think just one to three years out...is your product or service going to change dramatically or be obsolete? If yes, plan for it and innovate so you've created a path for potential buyers to offset their fear of obsolescence. A fearful or ignorant mind always says no. Take away their fear and educate your buyers.

CHAPTER 6

GROWTH

Imagine you're making your way through a jungle. You've got a big, sharp machete in hand, and you're hacking away at the obstacles in front of you. It's hard work, and you're sweaty and struggling through. You're moving forward, but only just.

Now imagine that you're with five other people, and all of them are in front of you doing the same thing. How much easier will your trek through the jungle be?

That's how buyers feel when you leave them a built-in path to growth. Eliminating obvious risk (Pillar #1) isn't enough. There has to be an upside for someone to buy your business—and that upside is growth.

Within the Growth Pillar, there are also six levels to think about:

1. Top-line trends

2. Bottom-line trends

3. Timing

4. Growth opportunities

5. Built-in paths to growth

6. Investments

TOP-LINE TRENDS

The first thing a buyer will look at for growth is what your revenue looks like year over year. The worst time to sell is when your numbers are lower than last year. Especially if the last few months are trending down compared to the same period last year. The message this gives buyers is that the next twelve months are going to be about fixing problems and rescuing the business, not riding the positive growth waves. If you are in this situation, wait until you can get the trends back upward if possible, or brace yourself for serious buyer concerns.

The actual numbers vary based on the business and how old it is. For a business that's about twenty-four months old, there should be a ton of growth year over year. It's in its infancy and should be just starting to take off. When we start edging toward five and six years old, 10–20 percent growth would still be positive, because it's coupled with the stability of an established business. The more growth relative to the stage the business is in, the bigger the buyer's incentive.

For the seller, a three- or four-time multiple is an excellent payday. For the buyer, it means it will take three or four years to break even if revenue stays flat. A business that's growing at 25 percent a year and selling at a 4x multiple, however, will get the buyer their money back in 2.7 years—assuming the 25 percent growth continues.

It is this kind of math that I wish more buyers would do. Instead, they go right for the list price multiple and decide to dig deeper—or, too often, not—on the multiple alone. The bottom line is that growth means buyers get to earn their money back faster, which makes them more comfortable paying a higher value. If you see a listing with a higher multiple, dig deeper and look at the growth trends. It could be because of incredible growth that will continue after the business transitions to the new owner.

BOTTOM-LINE TRENDS

There's a reason we started with top-line growth over the bottom line. I've seen people cut costs like crazy in the twelve months before they want to sell their businesses, attempting to maximize Seller's Discretionary Earnings. This will eventually catch up to you. If you stop advertising to minimize that expense, eventually the customers will stop showing up and that top-line revenue will go down as well.

"I know," people might say, "but I'm going to sell it."

Sure, but here's the thing: buyers can see through that. Buyers are smart. They've worked hard for their money and are cautious about spending it. They see when you're playing games. Booming bottom-line growth with declining top-line growth is a major red flag that something could be off. Trust is everything—and that type of approach will break that trust instantly.

TIMING

Two years ago, I sold a steadily growing business that earned 90 percent of its revenue in November and December. Their value came in around $2 million, and we sold it to a buyer who used SBA lending. If someone were to close on that business on January 1, they would have to struggle through ten months of a tenth of the revenue before getting a windfall, all the while making those sizable SBA payments. No one wants to start a new venture buying a business like that.

Instead, we focused on preparing the business for sale and listing it in the summer. That way, the buyer would get their windfall shortly after purchase to sustain them through the next year. We closed the transaction in mid-October, and by January 1 the buyer had a lot of money in his bank account.

Timing your sale with seasonal growth lets you hand off your business when it's at its peak, and that's appealing for a buyer. You're not trying to squeeze the last bit of revenue for yourself— you're preparing the business for the next person who will own it. Let them start on the upswing instead of at a disadvantage. If you try to sell just after your high seasonal peak, odds are it'll be a tougher sell, and it may not sell at all.

GROWTH OPPORTUNITIES

Let's say you sell privacy screens for computer monitors, and you've already created a SKU for every screen size and shape that's out there. How much growth does that leave for the next owner of the business?

Buyers aren't looking for an ATM that they pull some income from for a while. Most of the time, they want to make the investment, grow it, and eventually sell it for a higher value. For that to work, there has to be some untapped growth left.

What does your customer base look like? Is it a small total that you've already captured, or have you captured 2 percent of something enormous? If you don't know already, your buyer will find out for you.

Assuming the opportunity for growth exists, how clear is the path toward it? If you have sixteen stable SKUs, are there more that the buyer can launch over the next two to four years? If there are ten, do you have a path for the buyer to launch three more in the first twelve months?

Do you have a plan for the articles to be written in the future? If you've been reviewing vacuum cleaners for the last five years but you've never reviewed cordless vacuum cleaners, have you created a clear path to grow that niche?

What can you bolt onto your SaaS business that will keep customers coming back, paying more the next year, and the next, and the next?

In terms of getting people a solid return on their investments, these paths to growth are crucial. It's not just about the first year's revenue. This is a picture of the overall path the business is on. Making it clear makes the decision to buy that much easier—maybe even exciting.

BUILT-IN PATHS TO GROWTH

A few years ago, I sold a business with sixteen SKUs, seven of which had been launched in the six months prior to listing the business for sale. In just half the year, those seven SKUs already represented 20 percent of the total trailing twelve-month revenue. All the buyer had to do was close on the business and wait—all seven SKUs were going to create significant growth in the next few years. The path was clear, and it was already built in.

The buyer of that business tripled revenues in the twelve months after his purchase. The seller achieved his own financial goals and moved on. Sure, he may have left some money on the table, but he slept well at night, was debt free, and was able to move on to his next adventure unencumbered.

Any buyer would be hard-pressed to find a more exciting growth opportunity than one already cleared and built in. Don't be afraid to do some of the clearing for the next owner. Launch some new SKUs, add content, or tweak the code to boost monthly recurring revenue. Whatever your business model, buyers will love it more if there are *built-in* paths to growth.

INVESTMENTS

Often, someone will tell me they're thinking about doing a big push in a magazine to expand beyond the online world. B2B buyers might be looking at their products, and maybe a magazine pitched them a $25,000 offer. It sounds like a good investment. But I always ask a few probing questions. It usually goes like this:

"When will you make that investment and when will you get a ROI?"

"The ads launch in December and based on projections I should make a 2–3x ROI by the end of the following year."

When will we list the business for sale?

"I was hoping for February."

Really? Three months after an investment with a year-long ROI?

Think twice about making a substantial investment three months before you list. It could be a really good investment, but if you won't earn that money back while the business is still yours, skip it and let the buyer make the decision.

And here's how the math on that investment really works (*against you*):

- Invest $25,000

- ROI in twelve months, or about $2,083 per month

- Sell in three months and lose $18,750 of the investment ($2,083 × 9)

- Your listing multiple is 2.9x, so you've just lost 2.9 × $18,750 on the value of your business, or $54,375

- This advertising risk isn't worth it—don't do it

An exception to this rule is if the investment is a one-time investment and an add-back. No—advertising expenses are not add-backs. We cover that a bit later, in the Three Levels of Add-Backs.

Hold onto those opportunities and make them part of the growth plan for the coming year. You might even rank them in terms of potential return on investment, risk, cash outlay, the time it takes to get it back, and how much work it will take to make that investment. Then it becomes a path to growth that the buyer can choose, rather than something you've locked them into at no benefit, or negative benefit to yourself and potential risk to them.

This isn't to say you stop making investment choices entirely in the last year. Long-term brand building choices are different than something geared toward direct responses. For instance, if you invest in a software update that your current customer base will love, causing their stick rates to improve and their subscriptions to last longer, your monthly revenue will pop and it will be a smart investment. Or you might launch new SKUs and at the very least break even in the early months as the revenue grows.

Growth is one of the most important pillars. So, it is important to know yourself as an entrepreneur, know what you're capable of and good at and enjoy, and know when you need to move on. If you don't sell it when the business is growing, you're going to run into some painful roadblocks that could have been avoided.

Sell it while things are good, when the person who buys it will be excited to take it over. Then if you choose, you can do it all over again in a non-competing space in a new venture with more experience, excitement, motivation, and money.

ETHAN'S STORY

For about twelve months, I worked with a man named Marcus on a valuation plan for a business he was running alongside his full-time job. Stick with me.

It was a young business, but he had kept impeccable books. He was expanding SKUs, watching revenue trends, and doing everything just right. We were looking at a million-dollar exit, at least. Around the eight-month mark, we were much more comfortable working with each other and coming to the end of his plan when my phone rang.

"Hey, Joe. I want to talk for a minute. I actually have a confession to make."

I pulled my car over to the side of the road and listened.

"My name's not Marcus."

What?

"The first time I reached out to you, I was too paranoid to give you my real information. I made up a fake email address and have been lying to you this whole time, just in case. The good news is, everything else about my business is true. I just wasn't sure I could trust you. I'm sorry!"

It was a strange moment that I remember in vivid detail to this day—but what stands out even more is how smart he was about building his business. The week we listed it for sale he had a pre-planned adventure with his new bride, taking a three-month tour of the world. We went under letter of intent in less than ten days, and the buyer wound up flying to Hong Kong to meet with him during due diligence because that was the easiest place to meet up. I still have a picture of the two of them toasting to their new lives.

Ethan thought about the next owner from the beginning, and because of that foresight the buyer was able to triple the business inside of nine months. His own exit plan will put him in a position to never work again.

Growth matters, because being an EXITpreneur changes your life *and* the lives of others. Growth patterns are about what you're building for the next owner. Creating that opportunity becomes part of your legacy.

TIME OUT

- Run your P&L and see how last month's total revenues did compared to the same month last year. And then look at the last six months' average growth compared to the same period the previous year. You may still be growing, but is your growth slowing down? Don't wait to sell until growth has slowed dramatically or plateaued—buyers will punish you in the form of a reduced multiple.

- If your top-line revenue is shrinking and your SDE is growing, the reason should not be because you are cutting essential costs like advertising or key staff. Forget about being punished in the form of a lower multiple—this move will destroy trust and your business might not sell at all.

- When it comes to timing, sell when it is best for the buyer, not you. Get selfish and the likelihood of a clean and easy sale drops dramatically.

- Is growth tapped out or is there some left for your buyer? Create a growth vision and identify new content, upsell opportunities, SKUs, and channels of revenue that are realistic and achievable, and your buyer will reward you.

- Tap into some of your vision—don't just clear a path to one or more of the growth opportunities, but walk down that path and get the ball rolling. This creates a "built-in" path to growth that buyers love, so it's just a matter of continuing down the path you've opened up to boost their ROI.

- While growth is important, don't go for it at a substantial cost to the bottom line. If you are launching new SKUs, try to at least break even early on or minimize your losses. If you are planning on buying banner or print ads that won't give you a positive ROI for twelve months when you'll be selling in three, skip it and save that opportunity for your buyer. Losing $15,000 now when you're selling in three months could cost you $30,000 to $60,000 off your list price.

CHAPTER 7

....

TRANSFERABILITY

Suffice to say, if the assets driving the revenue of the business don't transfer, you really don't have a sellable business. It's as simple as that. If the primary assets that generate the revenue, traffic, reputation, and brand don't transfer to someone else, there's no point in someone buying it.

Again, there are six layers to understand in this pillar:

1. Key personalities

2. Key staff

3. Manufacturers

4. Contracts

5. Workload

6. Partners

KEY PERSONALITIES

A few months ago, I got to meet Alex, the Travel Fashion Girl.

Her story is incredible, and she's turned her travel blog into a profitable content and affiliate business. But it's not one that she can easily sell. People follow *her*. They love her updates and stories, and they trust her tips about traveling all over the world while packing light and keeping costs low. It centers around her, and that's not something a buyer can easily pick up.

If your name, personal reputation, or personal brand is a key driver for your business, it's not going to transfer easily. It can be done—you've just got to jump over a hurdle or three in order to make it work for the buyer. Alex is smart and loves what she does. And she has taken additional steps to build a business not fully dependent on her personality. She created a separate entity with a new line of travel accessories for all travelers as a solution. Alex can jump-start new travel-related product sales with her huge audience. But the brand's reputation is not fully dependent on her personality on an ongoing basis. Smart.

Now consider an e-commerce business in the cooking space. An owner wanted to publish videos that demonstrated the products, which helped with content development, traffic generation, affiliate revenue, and selling her own product. If she set up that channel as "Cooking with Jennifer," it would be all about her and less about the product or topic.

She could get creative—maybe "Cooking with Jennifers," where the gimmick is all guest hosts named Jennifer, or a neutral title with a caricature avatar instead of someone's actual face—but she couldn't make it about her without losing transferability.

In the past, I've seen entrepreneurs create transition periods where, over the course of six or twelve months after closing, the key person becomes less of a figure in the business. There's a risk there, though, which weaves into the first pillar and begins to weaken the whole deal.

If you're a key figure in the business, or if the key figure can't easily transfer over to someone else, do whatever you need to do to replace them now so your buyer won't have to worry about it later. Or, simply plan on selling the business while remaining the spokesperson during a longer than normal transition period. Put that in the teaser about your business for sale listing—that you'll stick around so the risk associated with losing you goes away. You can still get paid, unburden yourself of the day-to-day operations, and perhaps do what you love, which is to inspire others about your area of expertise.

KEY STAFF

When I sold my own business, I had a key employee who really made the business what it was, and I didn't want to let her know I was selling it. This became a significant risk for both me and my buyer. If she left beforehand, I would have been left holding the bag and my business would have been harder to sell. If she left after, the buyer would be in the same boat.

I waited until I was under Letter of Intent and part way through due diligence, with a much greater level of confidence that we were actually going to sell and close the transaction. Then I told her.

Naturally, she was afraid that the new buyer didn't want or need her. At the same time, the new buyer was worried *she* would leave, because that would mean needing to hire someone new. And *I* was concerned she wouldn't stick around, which could cause the sale to fall through.

To alleviate everyone's fears, I offered her a bonus paid out at three months and six months after I sold the business. I put it in an escrow fund to be released if she was still an employee at those times. She stuck around for another two years.

A recent SaaS business that I sold used a similar tactic for their key developer. We suggested talking with him in advance of the sale and incentivizing him to stick around by seeing if he wanted a future piece of the business. The buyer could offer 5 percent of the new company on top of his current salary, or provide a bonus on an annual basis for a certain period of time.

While the best way to alleviate those fears is to not have key staff in the first place, there are workarounds to be found.

When there are key employees who need to transfer with the business, it has to be taken care of. Consider all possible angles that might work for the employee and the new owners, including financial incentives, location, remote work, and personal considerations that might motivate them to stay.

MANUFACTURERS

The relationships and costs associated with the manufacturers you have now need to carry forward to the new owner of the business.

If your buyer has to go out and find a new manufacturer along with running a business they just purchased, perceived risk goes way up—and your value goes down. These existing relationships have to transfer. So do the terms.

Let's say you want to sell your nutritional supplement company, but the manufacturer planned to raise the prices for the new owner of the business within twelve months. When prices go up by a dollar a unit on something that used to make $20, your buyer will lose 5 percent of what they expected to be profit.

If that 5 percent equates to $10,000 ($200,000 in SDE × .05), your buyer may suggest your business is actually worth $30,000 less ($10,000 × a 3 multiple).

Number one, instill confidence. You're helping your buyer sort out their new future, so there's no reason to be defensive or rude about their concerns. You *know* your business and manufacturer, and they don't. Number two, remember that the manufacturer needs you *and* your buyer just as much as you need them. They're in business to be manufacturers and sell products or services to you, the owner of the business. It's a two-way street. And the reality is that your buyer will be excited and motivated to grow the business in ways you are not—this is good for the manufacturer!

These details can be tough to sort out, especially with overseas manufacturers and developers. The more you get strong relationships in place to make the transition smoother, the better it is for everyone involved.

CONTRACTS

The business that I sold carried a contract with a developer who received a small percentage of my total revenue every month. We had cut the deal early on, and it included a clause that indicated that if I sold the business, that contract would carry over to the new owner, and the percentage he received wouldn't change. This allowed the new buyer to take over the business in the exact same format. They could change or cancel the contract during its renewal, but because the contract transferred for an extended period of time after closing, the overall risk was low.

It's not always possible to have contracts carry over, especially with overseas companies. If you cannot get what you want in writing, do all you can to build the relationship so it is mutually beneficial and carries forward to a new owner with ease.

WORKLOAD

For businesses in the $50,000 to $20 million range—yes, that's an intentionally broad range—there is often a single point person who runs the business. This is fine and to be expected. But if you have two owners who are each working forty hours a week, it's not easily transferable to a single buyer. You need to revisit your workload to make it a reasonable, less-than-forty-hour week, or expect to only add back one owner's salary (we'll get to this in the all-important Three Levels of Add-Backs).

Your business will still be sellable if you work sixty or eighty hours a week, but you won't receive the same value for it as if you worked less. Buyers will have to plan to reduce that work-load and hire someone to do some of the work—and that comes at a cost. Start tracking those hours now to help identify alternatives. If twenty of your sixty hours are spent handling customer service, you can outsource that to a virtual assistant overseas who speaks English, is well-educated, and can do a great job for $4 or $5 an hour. If you let this be your buyer's problem, I promise they'll say, "We only hire Americans and pay no less than $15 an hour," even if it's not true. They are now dictating the cost and adjusting the overall value of your business on their terms, instead of yours.

PARTNERS

The sixth level is the transferability of partners. If one partner in the business has a non-transferable skill, you have to outsource it presale.

Your shared goal might be to sell the business, stick around for a short transition and training period, and then move onto the next adventure, but it'll be a difficult move if one of the partners is a developer who created the code from scratch. Your buyer may be a CEO, someone who will grow the business and has never done any coding, and they will have to hire someone to do what you do.

It's the same with being a great writer. If you write amazing 2,000-word articles on a particular subject for which you have a passion, skillset, and knowledge, you're going to be hard to replace. The buyer might be a Jack-of-all-trades-but-one, leaving them on the hook for hiring someone to catch up on that skill once you're gone.

Before you sell, you get to make those replacements and eliminate those fears before they're realized. Of course, if you're the partner who has that specific non-transferable skill, it's hard to know when to start outsourcing. Both partners have to be on the same page with an eventual exit date in mind.

This isn't terribly common. Maybe 5 percent of all transactions have this dynamic. But if that's you, remember that these businesses are generally valued off a multiple of the trailing *twelve* months. You should start planning for it at about six months out so that your replacement's work can be reflected in the metrics, as well as prove their mettle. They should have all the skills and operate on the same level you did. Give yourself time to make sure they're stable and ready so the buyer can take over with confidence.

TIME OUT

- If *you* are why people buy your product or service, you'll have to find a way to make the business less about you and more about the product or service itself. Or at the very least plan on sticking around as the spokesperson for the business after it sells. You've got to de-risk it for the buyers in order to get yourself maximum value.

- Key employees are key revenue drivers and must transfer with the business. Or at the very least—like the YOU above—stick around for a longer than normal transition period while replacements are found or developed.

- Manufacturer relationships, costs, and terms must carry forward to a new owner because they are part of what drives the bottom line. Do all you can to instill confidence in buyers so that this area of concern becomes a non-issue.

- Contracts are great, and you should get them wherever possible. Also accept when it is not possible, and build on the relationship to ensure breaking the news that you are selling comes easily and with no adverse impact to the business.

- Most sub-$20 million value online businesses are owner-operated. If you assume this will be your buyer, you cannot have two owners working eighty hours a week and expect your buyer to take over both roles. Outsource what you can at your cost of choosing, or your buyer will at a higher one and make you pay for it via the purchase price.

- The same goes for non-transferrable skills that an owner or partner has. Outsource the work at a cost determined by you and eliminate the unknown. If you don't, your buyer will see "risk" and overestimate the cost to replace you.

CHAPTER 8

DOCUMENTATION

In a recent valuation call, I listened as the entrepreneur described a business that sounded great. It was eleven years old and the company was paid through royalties on a monthly basis. They could provide the reports and they were willing to sell the business at a low value with a higher fee. Everything should have been in place and this seller's goals could be easily achieved. But when I asked for the profit and loss statement, the owner had absolutely nothing to give.

Without at least that basic form of documentation, the odds of that owner achieving their goals were incredibly low. If you want someone to stroke a check for a quarter of a million, a million, or ten million dollars, you have to give them the proper data to make a good investment decision. This is the number one reason people don't list their businesses—or don't sell after listing. They didn't have the data to instill confidence in the buyer.

Documentation comes in many forms, which we'll cover in another six categories:

1. Clear financials

2. Accrual accounting

3. Standard Operating Procedures (SOPs)

4. Contracts

5. Third-party reports

6. Metrics

CLEAR FINANCIALS

Good documentation starts with your financials—profit and loss statements (P&Ls) generated by a professional. The first step is to use standard bookkeeping software like QuickBooks or Xero, not just your own Excel sheets. They are standard, well-known accounting software programs that you can access online from anywhere in the world, and buyers have a higher trust for the documentation that comes from them.

The use of proper software instills confidence in buyers that you're a grownup who runs this business like a pro—thinking not just of yourself, but the buyer, who will be investing their life savings to buy it from you.

Using the right software is not all that should be done, though. The next step is to outsource the bookkeeping entirely, if you haven't already. Not you, not your friend, aunt, or mom, and not a full-time employee until they'd be doing much more than bookkeeping. Not even your CPA.

Each month, for less than the cost of a car payment (depending on the size of your business, of course), an e-commerce book-keeper will input (or import) all the data correctly using proper accounting and reconcile everything for you in your software account. Then you can run reports every month to analyze your business and focus on the big picture and how you are tracking toward your goals.

Ninety percent of the owners I talk to don't have these basic steps in place. When they bootstrapped the business, they threw it all together on an Excel spreadsheet and never looked back. No matter how accurate you are—remember Bob, from Chapter 2?—it won't be enough to get the buyer on board. Bob spent $1,500 to get everything in QuickBooks and verified, and earned $50,000 more than asking because of it.

Without good financials, we can't track any of the Key Metrics coming in Chapter 10, which means we can't verify the story of the business with math and logic. In short, the business would be nearly impossible to sell for the maximum value you deserve.

ACCRUAL ACCOUNTING

WAKE UP! I know—accounting makes your eyes bleed. But the most successful entrepreneurs endure and turn weaknesses into strengths.

The second level inside documentation is that you have to do accrual accounting, especially with an inventory-based business. This is how online businesses are sold. It benefits you because it presents your earnings more accurately. It benefits the buyer because it gives them an idea of what the real value of the business is. There's simply no justification for cash-basis accounting in almost any e-commerce business.

We covered the differences between cash and accrual in Chapter 3—along with a P&L example and how cash accounting hurts value. If you missed it, go back now and review.

Here is the formula for accrual accounting with regard to inventory:

(Beginning inventory + purchases) – ending inventory

Now take that dollar amount and divide it into the total revenue over the same period and you'll get your accrual percentage number.

That's the formula—but a good bookkeeper will take care of everything for you after some initial help from you. Occasionally I'll need to use this formula to "flip" COGS from cash to accrual in someone's P&L. But sometimes even doing this basic math is impossible because the business owner does not have accurate beginning and ending figures—either by month, year to date, or annually.

None of this work is easy. If it were, it wouldn't be so important. However, it is critical. Don't let anyone tell you anything different. If they do, odds are they are not telling you the full story. And just to be clear: if you are running an affiliate site or SaaS business, accrual accounting is just as important.

STANDARD OPERATING PROCEDURES (SOPS)

On the *Quiet Light* Podcast that I host with Mark Daoust, my business partner, one of the top episodes is an interview with a guy who has SOPs for his SOPs. His name is Norm Farrar (a.k.a. The Beard Guy), and he described for us exactly how important this kind of documentation can be, down to an SOP for how to make coffee in the office. SOPs are not just about being more efficient with our lives and time—they're about instilling confidence in the buyer.

If you've been launching upsells to your SaaS product or new SKUs, your SOPs on how to launch them should include screen recordings, step by step instructions, and any of the data needed to replicate the process. The new owner of the business should be able to review the SOPs and replicate the action fairly easily. Even if you need to show the owner how to do it, those SOPs will be there as a refresher each time they are needed—and you'll be needed less. Document each daily, repetitive task needed to run the business, using video (my current favorite platform for videos is Loom) wherever possible.

CONTRACTS AND THIRD-PARTY REPORTS

I've been self-employed for twenty-three years now, and for the longest time I would scramble to get my tax materials together for my CPA every spring. Eventually, I realized I could reconcile my finances every month, save my bank statements to a PDF inside of a folder, and then in January just share the link to that folder. My life—at least my tax season—got ten times easier after that.

The same is true when selling your business. Start saving all contracts, bank statements, merchant statements, third-party reports, and anything else that gives information about the revenue drivers of your business. Convert them to PDF, name them in a way that automatically sorts them in order, and file them away neatly in a folder on your computer, or better yet, in the cloud. When it's time for due diligence, you'll be able to hand over a main folder, with nested folders for each year and month, all ready to back up the financial claims you've made about the business.

ORGANIZATION PAYS OFF

This might sound like too much detail, but it helps to know how to make the files sort sequentially. Let's use the example of bank statements. If you were to just save them as Bank Statement or even "January Bank Statement," they would sort alphabetically or by the date last modified. That's less than helpful when you're trying to quickly review or verify numbers. Instead, label them as 1.2020, 2.2020, all the way through 12.2020. Organization to that level of detail helps the buyer do their due diligence better, which allows you to move on to the asset purchase agreement in a timely fashion, and eventually make it to the closing table. We'll get into this more in part IV, but the sooner you get organized, the easier those stages will be.

METRICS

This is another component that serves both you and your buyer. They are going to need to see certain metrics while they review the business, but the earlier you can track them, the better your business will be.

For example, if the lifetime value (LTV) of a customer increases, or the average cost to acquire (ACOS) a new customer jumps, or the return on ad spend (ROAS) is too high, the owner who is tracking metrics closely will know right away. You'll be able to catch problems before they blossom and pivot back toward a growth trend and your goals. As you improve the business incrementally, your value goes up. Then, when the buyers see your detailed metrics and their confidence goes up, the value goes with it.

In Chapter 10, we'll look closer at what those Key Metrics are.

THE GRIM REAPER'S STORY

There are times when my job makes an enormous difference in someone's life. They put together an excellent business, and I just have to advise them on the packaging, manage their emotions, and help them all along the way. Then we work out an incredible exit for them and they walk away appreciative and excited for the next time around.

Other times, I'm the grim reaper.

In one particular case, the gentleman said he'd almost signed an engagement letter with another firm, but changed his mind at the last minute. I was recommended to him, and based on what he told me, it sounded like we could make something work. His revenue was $10 million, with profits around $1.5 million, and he was looking for about $6 million from the sale. Based upon the risk and transferability, growth trends, diversification, etc., it sounded like a great business and an achievable goal.

But the financials were all wrong. The books were done on a cash basis with lots of adjustments and a lot of gaps. After a couple of weeks of painstaking data entry all by himself after we flipped it to accrual, his discretionary earnings dropped from $1.5 million to $800,000. A $700,000 difference played out over the multiple meant the business was worth maybe $3.2 million—far short of his $6 million goal.

It was crushing. Earlier that week, he had been optimistic and excited about finally getting his business listed. By Friday afternoon, I had to tell him there was no way we could achieve his goals. He wasn't lying at any point. He was just misinformed, and from that misinformation he set goals that weren't realistic. That's why we get the documentation right as early as possible—*you have to know where you are in order to get where you want to be.*

TIME OUT

- There are no substitutes for using the right accounting software. The standards are QuickBooks Online and Xero. Free options are available, but you do get what you pay for.

- Do NOT hire your CPA to do bookkeeping—they do tax planning and preparation. Hire an e-commerce bookkeeping firm. Go to EXITpreneur.io/Resources for a list of great e-commerce bookkeepers.

- Your P&L should be on an accrual basis, especially for a product business. Affiliate businesses too. Don't skip over this part. It is hard to set up, but it's a "must do" if you truly want to get maximum value for your business.

- Don't make light of being organized. Setting up SOPs and PDF copies of contracts impresses buyers and instills confidence. And that leads to higher values.

- Track your Key Metrics. When you closely track your own business Key Metrics, you can use that information to drive the business in the right direction—and toward your goals.

CHAPTER 9

THE FIFTH PILLAR THAT ISN'T

Risk, growth, transferability, and documentation are the four pillars, or what buyers want (and fear). There's no actual fifth pillar, as my business partner always reminds me. Except there kind of is. It's something very important that every buyer looks for, even if they can't name it. This magical, intangible, fifth non-pillar is the person behind the business.

You are the fifth pillar. Or at least the mortar that holds the four pillars together.

Businesses under LOI have fallen through because of the owners of those businesses. Businesses have sold at higher values than they should have because of the owners of those businesses.

The business is what it is, but only because you built it that way. If you want to sell it, you will be a factor in that deal. You need to be a professional. You need to be real and honest and trustworthy and likable and *good*.

If you want to be a great EXITpreneur, start by being a good human being.

ALL EYES ON YOU

The business looked nice on the surface. But within twenty-four hours, I got an odd email: "Hey, Joe, is this particular individual the owner of the business? If so, I'm out." Beneath the message was a link. It appeared that the business owner was a registered child sex offender.

This was a first for me, and I figured I had two options. One approach was telling the seller that I wasn't helping a registered child sex offender in any way, shape, or form. The other approach was to separate his past from this business and move forward as planned.

He hadn't brought this up with me first, so we were "getting ugly" way too far into the process. I had to ask him if the registered sex offender was, indeed, him. He told me a story that may or may not have been the truth. There's no way for me or anyone else to know. I had my own decisions to make, but it was ultimately the owner who had to wrestle with his past on display on the internet.

That incident was an odd one, but it's not the first time an owner's online records have undercut them. I have spoken with people who sound intelligent and professional on calls, but who plaster pictures all over social media of shirtless guys and bikini-clad women around a swimming pool drinking beers from funnels and partying it up.

The lesson is simple: in today's world, who you are and the way you behave outside of your business absolutely matters.

Everything is available to everyone, and most buyers *want* to find the dirt. Few people will sign a check for a million dollars to a forty-year-old frat kid. Put on a shirt, take your fun down from social media, and brace yourself for anything hidden to come to the surface. Because it will all be found, and it could shift the way buyers think of you.

BE A GOOD PERSON

On a recent deal we were almost through due diligence when it became clear that a portion of the inventory was old, tough to sell, and perhaps even unsellable.

Unprompted, my client (the owner of the business) sent me an email saying, "Hey, you know what? I've done a deep review of my own inventory aging reports, and I have several SKUs that I don't think I can sell at full price. I can't sell some of them at all. So I'm going to offer Matt (the buyer) a 30 percent discount for the ones that will eventually sell. For the other $10,000 worth of inventory that for the life of me, I can't sell, I will donate it to charity or he can have it—but he doesn't have to buy it."

Instead of trying to sell something that was overvalued, he did the right thing for his buyer before being asked. He built trust. And he wound up with a sold business because of it.

If you're a good person who's willing to go the extra mile and do what's necessary for your business, then be that person for your buyer, too. How you behave will help determine whether they're willing to risk their savings on you.

JOHN'S STORY

I became an Advisor at the tail end of the Great Recession. For the first two or three years, multiples were not climbing. Buyers were sensitive to every little detail, making the pillars more important than ever.

But that's exactly when I sold a seventeen-year-old content business for a much higher multiple than anything else at the time. The owner, John, had traveled the world with his wife, posting content wherever they went. They had subscribers and hosted contests. They earned money as affiliates through AdSense and Tribal Fusion revenue. He was seventy-two years old—mature, professional, charismatic, and likable. I wanted to be his friend, and I knew buyers would feel the same way. Even so, we were only able to push multiples to a certain level given the climate we were in. He disagreed. He said, "Joe, this business is worth more. I will talk to the buyers. You just get them on the phone with me and we'll sort this out."

It was a leap of faith. We were listing things at a max of a 2.74 multiple, so it would round down to 2.7 on our website—it took everything we had to get buyers interested in just about anything we listed for sale. Starting higher decreased John's chances of selling, and I told him that. But I also believed in him as a person. I liked and trusted him. We listed the business for a 4x multiple of his $400,000 in annual discretionary earnings. What should have been $1.1 million based on everyone's fears became $1.6 million—and he got it.

The only real reason for his success was that invisible fifth pillar. It was the person behind the business. This seller was so likable and trustworthy—and he'd created and operated a business that was great for the new owners to take over—that everyone who looked at it felt confident in it. Because people trusted him, they were willing to take more of a risk and pay more for it. He wound up with multiple offers. And it paid off for the buyers too—the seller was there for them in due diligence, and during the transition that came after closing. They've done well with the business since then, and the seller was able to enjoy retirement.

You matter just as much or even more than the business you're listing.

Update your LinkedIn profile. Clean up your Facebook page. Be careful what you say on Twitter. Be careful how you build, list, and sell your business. Create something great that another person will be happy to take over, and you'll both reap the rewards. That's the real value of your business. The numbers are fun, but what you and your buyer are able to do next—that's why we're in the game at all.

TIME OUT

- The person behind the business is nearly as important as the business itself.

- Think about your buyer and what's good for them as you build your business. Maximizing value doesn't mean just for you.

- Clean up your social media details. Avoid harsh political stances and images that are unsavory or show you in any way other than a likable, trustworthy entrepreneur.

PART III

RUNNING
THE PLAYS

CHAPTER 10

TRACK KEY FINANCIAL METRICS

After touching a half billion in transactions, I'm comfortable saying a review of certain financial Key Metrics is going to come up during every sale. They aren't just good to focus on—they are a window into the soul of the business. While you'll present the story of your business to the buyer, the metrics will lay out the math behind it. If your numbers were low last quarter, your story should explain that. If your story explains high and low points, the metrics should back it up. Ultimately, financial metrics are proof points that help your buyer trust you and understand your business.

If you hired a new CFO six months ago at $100,000 a year, the metrics should show the Seller's Discretionary Earnings decreasing a bit as a percentage of total revenues for the last six months. Math and logic.

In another scenario, you might explain to your buyer that you decided to give more responsibility to your virtual assistant in Q2. You let him run with some SOPs on the advertising budget, but then you took your eye off the ball. When you looked up three months later, your return on ad spend (ROAS) was down and ad cost was up. As soon as you caught the problem, you brought it back into focus and plan to keep your eye on the ball from now on. The SOPs are solid, and you've got a new VA on board who can handle it better. The financial Key Metrics should show the starting levels, the dip, and the shift as you pulled your attention back to the ad spend. Your story and the Key Metrics are all interwoven. Always.

After you identify the Key Metrics, start looking at them on a monthly basis. Just like the What Buyers Want—Four Pillars from Part II, tracking these metrics can also show you how to improve your business and prep it for the sale. Monitored well, they'll show you what's happening with competition, if you've screwed up at any point during the year, or if there's a negative blip in terms of discretionary earnings that needs attention. Metrics also help you know when it's time to sell.

For discretionary earnings of $250,000, a downward trend could drop the multiple from 3 to 2.8. This represents a $50,000 dip in the list price.

Let me lay that out for you:

$3 \times \$250,000 = $ a list price of $750,000

$2.8 \times \$250,000 = $ a list price of $700,000

You just lost $50,000 because of downward trends and a late focus on "deciding" to sell, instead of "preparing" to sell.

For the average entrepreneur who just decides to sell, you'll miss the opportunities to bring that multiple back up, or you'll be too worn out to make the change even if you see what needs to be done. Since you're not passionate or excited about the business anymore, you're now down both emotionally and financially.

The EXITpreneur is watching these metrics all the time, at least six to eighteen months in advance of when they want to sell. You're preparing (training) to exit, so you'll be able to do the work to move those numbers up *before* you list, putting $50,000 or more back in your pocket on closing day.

Finally, when they're all tracked and aligned to the story, financial Key Metrics can alleviate some of the concerns that invariably show up in the pillars. Risks and weak areas sometimes make more sense when the metrics demonstrate logic and reason behind them.

For example, a four-year-old business with a hero SKU doing 50 percent of the total revenue doesn't sound great. But if it's grown by 150 percent in the trailing twelve months, that dramatic year-over-year growth may offset some of the risk that comes from a hero SKU alone. All of these factors play into each other to help buyers assess the value of a business and what they can do with it.

To maximize your opportunity, there are four primary financial Key Metrics to track:

1. Total revenue trends

2. Gross profit trends

3. Advertising trends

4. Seller's discretionary earnings (SDE) trends

Using math and numbers, demonstrated visually with charts and stories, we can create a complete picture of your business that helps buyers make their decision with confidence.

TOTAL REVENUE TRENDS

A colleague of mine, Chris Yates, owns an online due diligence firm called Centurica. They help buyers make sure that the financials of the businesses they buy are accurate. Chris says that a frequent red flag they spot is when a buyer brings him the financials for the business they are buying, and they are presented on an annual, quarterly, or six-month only basis, compared to the previous period. At that point, there's a very high chance that the owner or Broker of that business is hiding something.

When buying an online business, you can look at annual and quarterly trends, but then the numbers should always be available to be viewed on a month-to-month basis.

How this month compares to last month isn't always important. It's how this month compares to the same month last year. Buyers generally want something that is trending up with seasonality in mind.

CHARTING OUT YOUR METRICS

I have created Google Sheets that I share to help you track your own Key Metrics. I also walk through the formulas with example P&Ls and share what the "Key Metrics say" to buyers in those P&Ls. Visit EXITpreneur. io/Resources to grab your copy.

You also don't need to worry if the fourth quarter does really well but then business falls off a bit in January, as long as the business did the same thing last year. That doesn't hurt these trends or necessarily indicate that it's a bad time to sell. Every buyer will take seasonality into account, and the monthly analysis will demonstrate those seasonal shifts in light of the overall trends.

The best time to sell is when the revenues are up the last few months compared to the same few months last year. The worst time to sell is when the last two or three months are weak compared to the same months in the previous year.

In the example of the 3 to 2.8 time multiple, even if you thought about listing the business twelve months in advance and managed to steady the numbers, you still only have something worth $750,000. But if you're tracking Key Metrics, you'll know what might increase that multiple or bring it down. You'll know how significant a two-tenths change could be for a business with $250,000 in discretionary earnings, and focus on some small things that could add tens of thousands in value to your list price.

The more you know and track, the more you'll be able to earn on your exit. And if we get twelve months out and your business is, in fact, worth a million dollars, you don't have to sell if you don't want to. If you love it, just keep doing what you're doing. You're learning so much, and you have an asset that's growing and sellable. Alternatively, your goal of exiting in eighteen months for a million dollars may be achievable in fifteen months if your growth has been accelerated. If everything I've talked about is in place, then you can jump on an upward trend and list even earlier.

Chapter 10: Year-over-Year Key Metrics Snapshot

Year-over-Year Revenue Trends

	Feb	Mar	Apr	May	Jun	Jul	Aug	Sep	Oct	Nov	Dec	Jan	Total
2017–18	83,213	72,781	25,364	13,699	23,448	13,279	56,589	61,084	81,676	149,199	221,724	110,676	912,732
2018–19	101,116	137,581	114,705	108,851	83,645	125,338	83,700	123,834	132,204	224,725	309,435	139,216	1,684,349
2019–20	119,725	149,970	101,002	94,988	104,754	177,306	218,979	156,701	192,283	310,787	556,032	251,430	2,433,956
TTM % Chg.	18%	9%	-12%	-13%	25%	41%	162%	27%	45%	38%	80%	81%	45%

With the above sample business buyers will see overall positive trends with YOY growth up 45 percent. Note the two negative growth months in April and May of 2019. This could be because of inventory issues or that VA that took over advertising, doing a poor job before the owner spotted the problem. Without a clear view of these Key Metrics, issues can drag on and be very costly while running the business—and even more so when you exit.

GROSS PROFIT TRENDS

Each metric is its own device and should be tracked carefully based on its objectives. In this case, we're comparing the last twelve months to the previous twelve months to see if gross profit is going up or down. We can look at gross profit in two different ways: (1) in dollars, and (2) as a percentage of total revenue. Both are necessary to track. Buyers often look to see if margins are being squeezed by competition (reducing prices) or if COGS is going up because your manufacturer's costs have gone up. Your gross profit as a percentage of total revenue will tell buyers a lot—and should back up what you say in a written or recorded interview about your business and its trends.

Both also underscore another key moment for accrual-based accounting. If you bought $100,000 in inventory one month and zero the next month and used cash accounting, your gross profit as both a percentage of total revenue and as dollars would be all over the place. This could hurt you as the seller by skewing your overall discretionary earnings—and remember, even 5 percent can represent tens of thousands in value. Not to mention that it would hurt a buyer if the timing fell so that the COGS appears lower than it actually was. Buyers can pay too much or too little with just a minor shift of this metric, so be careful to get it right.

Chapter 10: Gross Profit in $ and % Key Metrics Snapshot

Gross Profit in Dollars

	Feb	Mar	Apr	May	Jun	Jul	Aug	Sep	Oct	Nov	Dec	Jan	Total
2017–18	49,629	35,685	10,807	5,807	15,521	6,030	30,669	29,090	41,986	79,490	111,875	48,544	465,135
2018–19	49,009	64,051	53,028	51,932	37,116	45,446	31,825	46,094	50,715	92,160	118,197	53,399	692,972
2019–20	76,860	97,995	67,410	59,825	69,394	123,131	144,263	104,542	133,138	216,073	384,548	162,256	1,639,435
TTM % Chg.	57%	53%	27%	15%	87%	171%	353%	127%	163%	134%	225%	204%	137%

Gross Profit as a % of Total Revenue

	Feb	Mar	Apr	May	Jun	Jul	Aug	Sep	Oct	Nov	Dec	Jan	Total
2017–18	60%	49%	43%	42%	66%	45%	54%	48%	51%	53%	50%	44%	51%
2018–19	48%	47%	46%	48%	44%	36%	38%	37%	38%	41%	38%	38%	41%
2019–20	64%	65%	67%	63%	66%	69%	66%	67%	69%	70%	69%	65%	67%
TTM % Chg.	32%	40%	44%	32%	49%	92%	73%	79%	80%	70%	81%	68%	64%

Hmmmm. A buyer may look at this and wonder why total revenues are up just 45 percent (see the YOY Total Revenue image) and gross profit is up a whopping 137 percent in dollars, with 64 percent as a percentage of total revenues.

Could it be this business owner renegotiated and reduced COGS on some or all top-selling SKUs? Or is it because the previous year was a challenging one, and they met with an Advisor to help them get the business in great shape for a great buyer to take over at a great price? Note that gross profit as a percentage of total revenues looks consistent in the last twelve months. From February of 2018 through January of 2019, they were as low as 37 percent and as high as 48 percent. So perhaps it was a combination of both.

Buyers love analyzing these Key Metrics because it gives them the full picture of the business. When a business owner has access to and analyzes the Key Metrics regularly, they can pivot and adjust as needed to make sure they stay on track to their goals. Fly blind and, well, you can't see.

ADVERTISING TRENDS

A recent client sold his business that was in a product category that he used personally. The idea for it came from a product he bought from someone else, but it's a product that's very uncomfortable to the point where he didn't wear it enough, even though he wanted to wear it for safety reasons. Since the product wasn't patented, he came up with a better, more comfortable variation of that product and let friends and family try it too. Everyone raved about it. When he launched it on his website and Amazon, it took off with organic rankings and reviews with just a small advertising budget.

His business grew so fast that he put almost all the cash right back into buying more inventory just to keep up. Because he only spent about 3 percent of the total revenue on advertising, there was a lot more room for opportunity that he didn't capture. He just didn't have the expertise, nor did he want to hire out for it. But the company that bought the business did exactly that. They spent more, so they obtained more customers with the same ACOS (average cost of sale).

In advertising trends in particular, buyers who discover only 3 percent of the total revenue is spent on advertising learn a lot about what you've built and what they might build on. Bootstrapped EXITpreneurs who don't have a lot of online marketing experience work hard, hustle, and have to take a certain amount out of the business to live off of, so they may keep things really tight. You had a great idea but didn't have the online marketing experience or financial bandwidth that could take it to the next level. Buyers who want to start with something solid and take it to the next level don't often share those constraints.

With content sites, SaaS businesses, and e-commerce businesses, there are general ranges where you'll want to fall within each of these Key Metrics. For an e-commerce business in which the majority of the revenue comes from a website, gross profit will be a higher percentage of total revenue than if the majority of revenue was from Amazon, because the platform fees are higher with Amazon. Ad costs may be higher with a website revenue-driven business, though—and ad costs fall below the gross profit line. In about 50 percent of P&Ls I review, the platform fees are above the gross profit line with FBA-based businesses. I cannot say if there is a right or wrong way with this, as FBA businesses are relatively new and bookkeepers have not set standard practices yet.

Generally speaking, for advertising as a percentage of total revenue, we see it range anywhere from 5 percent to 20 percent, though the latter gets a little rich when you have platform fees for an FBA business. A content site might not have any advertising, because they're really just focused on good quality content and rankings with SEO.

Again, we want to track the metrics when they're great *and* when they hurt—what's ugly for you can be an opportunity for your buyer, or an opportunity for you to improve your business to get it ready to sell. This isn't about smoothing out the rough edges, but about painting a clear picture of the business as it is.

Chapter 10: Advertising in $ and % Key Metrics Snapshot

Advertising Dollars

	Feb	Mar	Apr	May	Jun	Jul	Aug	Sep	Oct	Nov	Dec	Jan	Total
2017–18	1,032	1,938	7,651	2,774	3,502	2,528	6,844	11,221	17,173	27,779	34,903	23,307	140,651
2018–19	17,950	23,381	17,418	15,187	14,240	12,176	14,017	24,928	30,048	43,051	36,544	29,796	278,733
2019–20	19,947	16,037	8,893	8,770	15,614	18,470	27,721	15,952	11,464	16,929	29,986	20,617	210,400
TTM % Chg.	11%	-31%	-49%	-42%	10%	52%	98%	-36%	-62%	-61%	-18%	-31%	-25%

Advertising as % of Revenue

	Feb	Mar	Apr	May	Jun	Jul	Aug	Sep	Oct	Nov	Dec	Jan	Total
2017–18	1%	3%	30%	20%	15%	19%	12%	18%	21%	19%	16%	21%	15%
2018–19	18%	17%	15%	14%	17%	10%	17%	20%	23%	19%	12%	21%	17%
2019–20	17%	11%	9%	9%	15%	10%	13%	10%	6%	5%	5%	8%	9%
TTM % Chg.	-6%	-37%	-42%	-34%	-12%	7%	-24%	-49%	-74%	-72%	-54%	-62%	-48%

In this example, advertising as a percentage of total revenue jumps to over 20 percent in September and October of 2019. Perhaps this is in preparation for Christmas sales, or perhaps it is because a VA took over ad spending and did a poor job. The Key Metrics view in this format will allow both a seller and buyer to analyze the business trends for sources of risk and improvement.

As an Advisor, I'd want to make sure advertising was not cut to boost SDE at the last moment. At a glance this P&L certainly says that could be what's going on. But then again, total revenue *is* up by 45 percent, so organic traffic could be up, or conversion rates could be higher. I'd ask that question and make the answer available to buyers so they can move on with the next step with confidence.

Either way, Key Metrics are a window into the soul of a business and tell the full story, or at least raise questions that can be answered to get that story—and help you sell your business for a great value to a solid buyer.

SELLER'S DISCRETIONARY EARNINGS TRENDS

Seller's Discretionary Earnings trends should also track in both dollars and as a percentage of total revenue. If your total revenue is up but your SDE are flat year over year, your margins have shrunk and the business needs to be priced accordingly. Try to hide this fact and your deal will get renegotiated—or fall apart in due diligence, making all of your work for nothing.

Imagine two businesses being sold, both generating half a million dollars in SDE, but for the first business, that half million is only 5 percent of the total revenue. For the second business, it's 20 percent. If the earnings shift down a bit in the 20 percent SDE business, it won't have as dramatic an impact on the bottom line as in the business with tighter margins.

With the 20 percent SDE business, a 1 percent change is $25,000. With the 5 percent SDE business, a 1 percent change is $100,000, a $75,000 difference. The difference is significant enough that any time the bottom-line percentage is low overall, it's a red flag and a serious concern for buyers. This takes us back to the Risk Pillar in Chapter 5.

Here's another situation commonly reflected in this metric: inventory outages. Almost every rapidly growing e-commerce business occasionally runs out of inventory. When that happens, you'll see a drop in the total revenue key metric, the gross profit, *and* the SDE.

For business owners, it's easy to think, "I normally make X percentage, but I ran out of inventory that particular month. I'll just do an add-back of $20,000 in discretionary earnings because that's what Amazon tells me I would have earned if I had the inventory." Neither the math nor the logic works for buyers there. We'll cover this in detail in Chapter 11, when we review the Three Levels of Add-Backs.

Every dramatic shift in a metric tells a story that helps buyers make an informed decision. What you see as a negative could be an opportunity for the right buyer. For a buyer who knows they're good at managing inventory levels, inventory outage information is vital. They'll come to the business with more working capital and maybe five months instead of three months of inventory on hand.

Did you spend more money? Did you hire two more developers or writers? Did you have tariffs? Did your freight costs go up? Did you repackage the product or add something to it that increased your cost of goods sold? Did that change also reduce your return rates and increase your review count to make it worth it? Maybe your cost of goods sold changed because of freight or tariff increases, or you're not spending your advertising dollars as efficiently, or you have to spend more money because organic rankings dropped. Whenever you're driving more revenue but discretionary earnings are down, it's an indicator that you need to pay attention. Something is off and needs to be addressed. Studying your own Key Metrics will help you make informed decisions to drive your business toward your exit goals.

Chapter 10: Seller's Discretionary Earnings in $ and % Key Metrics Snapshot

Seller's Discretionary Earnings (SDE)

	Feb	Mar	Apr	May	Jun	Jul	Aug	Sep	Oct	Nov	Dec	Jan	Total
2017–18	31,155	22,232	-10,635	-8,123	-2,180	-11,329	10,116	4,058	6,438	31,969	48,375	12,545	134,621
2018–19	6,200	23,874	17,198	20,243	9,984	15,910	5,729	7,857	10,826	27,904	66,517	11,002	223,242
2019–20	9,185	19,417	6,707	13,951	5,844	15,370	35,841	24,561	32,750	60,281	120,736	48,253	392,896
TTM % Chg.	48%	-19%	-61%	-31%	-41%	-3%	526%	213%	203%	116%	82%	339%	76%

Seller's Discretionary Earnings (SDE) as % of Revenue

	Feb	Mar	Apr	May	Jun	Jul	Aug	Sep	Oct	Nov	Dec	Jan	Total
2017–18	37%	31%	-42%	-59%	-9%	-85%	18%	7%	8%	21%	22%	11%	15%
2018–19	6%	17%	15%	19%	12%	13%	7%	6%	8%	12%	21%	8%	13%
2019–20	8%	13%	7%	15%	6%	9%	16%	16%	17%	19%	22%	19%	16%
TTM % Chg.	25%	-25%	-56%	-21%	-53%	-32%	139%	147%	108%	56%	1%	143%	22%

Compared with August of 2019, the SDE for this business is up dramatically. What happened in August to make this shift? A launch of a new upsell? An article that drove more traffic? Or did that investment in conversion rate optimization (CRO) finally pay off for this business owner? Without a clear view of these Key Metrics, a business owner or buyer won't know what questions to ask or what projects to focus on in order to achieve their goals.

Here are all of the Key Metrics in one view. Study them. Look at the shifts in total revenues and the correlating ad spend. What impact did it have on SDE and does it compute using math and logic? Are there questions that come up that need answers based on these numbers?

If you are a buyer, you could create this Key Metrics tab for the businesses you are considering buying to make a much more informed decision. If you are a seller studying your own business's Key Metrics, you'll see the big picture created by many little details. These are the details you control and can adjust and tweak as you drive toward your goals.

Chapter 10: Financial Key Metrics: Example Business

	Feb	Mar	Apr	May	Jun	Jul	Aug	Sep	Oct	Nov	Dec	Jan	Total
Year Over Year Revenue Trends													
2017–18	83,213	72,781	25,364	13,699	23,448	13,279	56,589	61,084	81,676	149,199	221,724	110,676	912,732
2018–19	101,116	137,581	114,705	108,851	83,645	125,338	83,700	123,834	132,204	224,725	309,435	139,216	1,684,349
2019–20	119,725	149,970	101,002	94,988	104,754	177,306	218,979	156,701	192,283	310,787	556,032	251,430	2,433,956
TTM % Change	**18%**	**9%**	**-12%**	**-13%**	**25%**	**41%**	**162%**	**27%**	**45%**	**38%**	**80%**	**81%**	**45%**
Gross Profit in Dollars													
2017–18	49,629	35,685	10,807	5,807	15,521	6,030	30,669	29,090	41,986	79,490	111,875	48,544	465,135
2018–19	49,009	64,051	53,028	51,932	37,116	45,446	31,825	46,094	50,715	92,160	118,197	53,399	692,972
2019–20	76,860	97,995	67,410	59,825	69,394	123,131	144,263	104,542	133,138	216,073	384,548	162,256	1,639,435
TTM % Change	**57%**	**53%**	**27%**	**15%**	**87%**	**171%**	**353%**	**127%**	**163%**	**134%**	**225%**	**204%**	**137%**
Gross Profit as a % of Total Revenue													
2017–18	60%	49%	43%	42%	66%	45%	54%	48%	51%	53%	50%	44%	51%
2018–19	48%	47%	46%	48%	44%	36%	38%	37%	38%	41%	38%	38%	41%
2019–20	64%	65%	67%	63%	66%	69%	66%	67%	69%	70%	69%	65%	67%
TTM % Change	**32%**	**40%**	**44%**	**32%**	**49%**	**92%**	**73%**	**79%**	**80%**	**70%**	**81%**	**68%**	**64%**
Advertising Dollars													
2017–18	1,032	1,938	7,651	2,774	3,502	2,528	6,844	11,221	17,173	27,779	34,903	23,307	140,651
2018–19	17,950	23,381	17,418	15,187	14,240	12,176	14,017	24,928	30,048	43,051	36,544	29,796	278,733
2019–20	19,947	16,037	8,893	8,770	15,614	18,470	27,721	15,952	11,464	16,929	29,986	20,617	210,400
TTM % Change	**11%**	**-31%**	**-49%**	**-42%**	**10%**	**52%**	**98%**	**-36%**	**-62%**	**-61%**	**-18%**	**-31%**	**-25%**

Chapter 10: Financial Key Metrics: Example Business (cont'd)

	Feb	Mar	Apr	May	Jun	Jul	Aug	Sep	Oct	Nov	Dec	Jan	Total
Advertising as % of Revenue													
2017–18	1%	3%	30%	20%	15%	19%	12%	18%	21%	19%	16%	21%	15%
2018–19	18%	17%	15%	14%	17%	10%	17%	20%	23%	19%	12%	21%	17%
2019–20	17%	11%	9%	9%	15%	10%	13%	10%	6%	5%	5%	8%	9%
TTM % Change	**-6%**	**-37%**	**-42%**	**-34%**	**-12%**	**7%**	**-24%**	**-49%**	**-74%**	**-72%**	**-54%**	**-62%**	**-48%**
Seller's Discretionary Earnings (SDE)													
2017–18	31,155	22,232	-10,635	-8,123	-2,180	-11,329	10,116	4,058	6,438	31,969	48,375	12,545	134,621
2018–19	6,200	23,874	17,198	20,243	9,984	15,910	5,729	7,857	10,826	27,904	66,517	11,002	223,242
2019–20	9,185	19,417	6,707	13,951	5,844	15,370	35,841	24,561	32,750	60,281	120,736	48,253	392,896
TTM % Change	**48%**	**-19%**	**-61%**	**-31%**	**-41%**	**-3%**	**526%**	**213%**	**203%**	**116%**	**82%**	**339%**	**76%**
Seller's Discretionary Earnings (SDE) as % of Revenue													
2017–18	37%	31%	-42%	-59%	-9%	-85%	18%	7%	8%	21%	22%	11%	15%
2018–19	6%	17%	15%	19%	12%	13%	7%	6%	8%	12%	21%	8%	13%
2019–20	8%	13%	7%	15%	6%	9%	16%	16%	17%	19%	22%	19%	16%
TTM % Change	**25%**	**-25%**	**-56%**	**-21%**	**-53%**	**-32%**	**139%**	**147%**	**108%**	**56%**	**1%**	**143%**	**22%**

JENNIFER'S STORY

When Jennifer and I went over her metrics for the business she hoped to sell, we found a problem in her trailing twelve months. She had trained a virtual assistant to take care of ad spend, then turned to focus on other things. With her attention elsewhere, her cost per order started to creep up as her return on ad spend went down. When we looked at the metrics all together, that three-month period created a $20,000 *increase* in ad spend with no bump in revenue.

With the numbers on full display, Jennifer did some digging to find the root of the problem. Turns out, the assistant had simply not followed the SOPs she trained him on. She couldn't afford further increases, so she took the job back and brought her attention back to her advertising costs.

When we listed Jennifer's business, this entire story was told in two places: the written client interview and the advertising Key Metrics. In the interview, she explained the mistakes and how she remedied them. In the metrics, we could see the typical ad spend, then an increase and peak over those three months, then a drop back down to original levels once she resolved it.

Unfortunately for Jennifer, some of that extraneous ad spend was completely lost. If even 50 percent of it was a waste, that's $10,000 off the bottom-line SDE. At her 3x multiple, taking her eyes off the metrics for ninety days lost her as much as $30,000 off the list price. She took a mental break from the financials and it hurt badly. But—with the clear picture these Key Metrics showed us and the buyers—we were able to increase Jennifer's multiple to offset the mistake she made with the VA, and offset some of her losses. The data intertwined with the backstory instilled confidence and trust with the buyers and they were willing to pay the slight bump in the multiple.

I've seen it in ad spend, developer costs, and shipping fees. A friend of mine watched his shipping costs creep up by a few percentages each month for a few months in a row, all because of a minor mistake made by the freight company. Without tracking his metrics to find that error, in just a year he calculated a potential million dollars lost in SDE. His business eventually sold for a 10x multiple. If he had not focused on reviewing his Key Metrics and P&Ls monthly, this mistake would have cost him $10 million.

I don't blame you for struggling with your numbers. You're an EXITpreneur, not a bookkeeper or an accountant, and even if you *are* one of these in some facet of your life, you're not one in this context. Most of us are drinking opportunities through a firehose. We're doing everything we can do to keep up with the growth of the business and fight off competition and learn new channels. We are good at growing the business—but what we need to get better at is quantifying that growth.

Far too many business owners hit that $1 to 5 million mark without actually putting much money in their personal bank account. Far too many struggle to track the everyday numbers themselves rather than handing it over to a bookkeeper and freeing their brain to track the Key Metrics. Far too few of them review a detailed profit and loss statement on an accrual basis regularly throughout the year. Far too few project the true value of the business for an intentional exit.

Tread water like that for long enough, and you'll run out of energy. We can always get rid of something. Intentionally selling it for what it's worth is another story.

We can always drive revenue. Turning that revenue into an upward trend of Seller's Discretionary Earnings is another story.

There's nothing sexy or fun about planning, training, or preparing. There's nothing sexy or fun about metrics. But when it's time to sell, you'll be much better off with impressive top-line numbers in a well-managed, well-tracked business than if you just rolled with the punches. With your metrics in place, you'll spot the ideal time to sell, exit well, and start over again with a million or two or ten in the bank, and a wealth of knowledge to help you reach even bigger heights next time. Some consider that *very* sexy after all.

TIME OUT

- "Revenue is vanity, profits are sanity"—Dave Bryant and Mike Jackness from EcomCrew say this often. And it's true. Track all of your Key Metrics, not just your total revenue numbers.

- A small $1,000 mistake in the twelve months prior to selling could cost you $3,000–$5,000 off your list price. A $10,000 mistake = $30,000–$50,000. Closely track everything in the months prior to listing the business for sale.

CHAPTER 11

IDENTIFY ALL YOUR ADD-BACKS

Of the thousands of profit and loss statements that I've reviewed over the years, no two are ever alike. Entrepreneurs, bookkeepers, and CPAs are all doing things slightly-to-very differently, and the combination of variables means every P&L is unique and needs interpretation. It means we have to comb the financials closely, with an expert eye, to make sure we aren't overvaluing or leaving money on the table (which is usually the case).

What is the definition of an add-back?

An add-back is an owner benefit, accounting (non-cash) or one-time, non-recurring expense that will not carry forward to the new owner of the business. It could also be an adjustment that reflects the new normal that is only partly reflected in the trailing twelve-month P&L. Add-backs help us present the true, clear, and accurate Seller's Discretionary Earnings of the business for potential acquirers. This is not EBITDA (Earnings Before Interest, Taxes, Depreciation, and Amortization). It's more along the lines of Adjusted EBITDA because it takes into account single owner-operator salaries and perks, along with a host of other legitimate adjustments.

The biggest mistake I see entrepreneurs make when selling their business—on their own or through an inexperienced Advisor—is not doing a thorough review of add-backs. It's easy to lose tens of thousands of dollars in value without a deep dive into add-backs. It's also easy to gain instant equity as a buyer, either when buying direct or with an inexperienced Advisor helping the seller.

To cover their bases, I have all of my clients work through the Three Levels of Add-Backs. The first two are a bit more obvious, and the third is much more variable in nature. For each level of add-backs, we'll touch on a range of potential areas to analyze. The goal isn't to fabricate an add-back for every item, but to understand your business from every possible angle.

Some P&Ls have a lot of add-backs and others have very few. I've listed and sold a business or two with fifteen-plus lines of add-backs that add up to more than the net income. It only worked because the math and logic were clear and were backed up by third-party statements, the financial Key Metrics, and the owner's story.

If you rush through the add-back process you will absolutely lose value. If you push too hard and start stretching the logic, you will lose trust. This is where math and logic shine, and it's one of my favorite things to talk about.

Like the Four Pillars of Value, each of the Three Levels of Add-Backs has six sublevels. Let's take a look.

LEVEL ONE ADD-BACKS: THE OBVIOUS

1. One Owner's Salary

2. Owner Health Insurance and Retirement Contributions

3. Amortization

4. Depreciation

5. Charitable Contributions

6. Interest Expenses

ONE OWNER'S SALARY

The first, most obvious owner benefit is owner payroll. If an owner-operator's business shows a net income of exactly zero dollars, but the owner takes a $300,000 salary, does that mean the business is worth zero? No, you add back the owner's salary—below the net income line—to the add-back schedule, boosting SDE by $300,000 in this case.

There are exceptions to every rule, and this applies to owner salary as well. If you work sixty hours a week, you cannot do a simple 100 percent add-back, because it's not a reasonable expectation for the new owner to work sixty hours a week. That is generally not what they are looking for. Just as we had to create a long-term plan for this scenario in the Four Pillars, we have to consider it for add-backs as well.

Without planning in advance, you won't be able to find a way to reduce your workload, and/or offload more time-consuming but menial tasks to a virtual assistant at a much lower cost. As previously discussed, there are a number of talented VAs living overseas at lower costs of living who work for remarkably low rates.

For that $300,000 and a steady sixty-hour week, the buyer won't consider it a 100 percent add-back. They'll want to hire someone for at least twenty hours a week at $30,000 a year. At a 3x multiple, they'll offset the overall value and drop their offer by $90,000 using their own math and logic. Their math may not make sense to you, but you left this up to them by not preparing to sell and outsourcing some of your work to a VA at $5 an hour.

The same applies for two owners. Only one forty-hour-week salary is considered a direct add-back. This is especially true if one of the owners has a non-transferable skill, or one that is specialized like programming or coding. If that's you, I'd suggest you outsource this work to someone with the necessary skills and at a cost that works for you. If you leave this up to your buyer, they'll inflate the cost and reduce their offer by that amount times the multiple your business is listed for. And that could cost you tens of thousands at closing.

OWNER HEALTH INSURANCE AND RETIREMENT CONTRIBUTIONS

Neither of these expenses carries forward to the new owner of your business. And even if the new owner did choose to run their health insurance through the business, they could have easily opted out and chose coverage under their spouse's company benefits.

The same goes for owner retirement contributions. These are definitely not carry-forward expenses. A new owner may choose to make contributions through the company, but how much and how often is completely optional.

AMORTIZATION

According to Investopedia.com, amortization is an accounting term that refers to the process of allocating the cost of an intangible asset over a period of time. It also refers to the repayment of loan principal over time. Because this intangible asset, or loan, does not carry forward in a sale, it is an add-back as well. Both amortization and depreciation are part of EBITDA, or Earnings Before Interest, Taxes, Depreciation, and Amortization. I rarely see them on P&Ls provided by people using professional bookkeepers or doing the books on their own.

DEPRECIATION

Depreciation is a reduction in the value of an asset that occurs over time as the asset gets older or as wear and tear occurs. Your bookkeeper or CPA may add this "non-cash" expense to your P&L because they can within the tax code. This is why real estate investors pay so little in taxes. It helps you too, but to a much lesser degree. It is still an add-back because it is not a real cash expense, nor one that carries forward.

CHARITABLE CONTRIBUTIONS

This is in level one because it should be fairly obvious that an owner's choice to contribute to charity is not a carry-forward expense that the new owner will incur. Again though, there are exceptions to every rule.

Example: I once sold a company that donated one dollar for every "made in the USA cutting board" that was sold, to a non-profit that would plant ten new trees for each dollar donated. Annually this accounted for about $50,000 in charitable contributions. Because the marketing efforts centered around these charitable donations and helped drive sales, the $50,000 would not be considered an add-back.

If I had been able to speak with these owners well in advance of their decision to sell their business, I may have suggested doing a split test to determine if the charitable donation marketing efforts truly resulted in more sales—enough that a $50,000 annual expense was acceptable. If the split test resulted in no difference, it's easy math to see that a 3.5x multiple adds $175,000 to the list price of their business when they sell.

INTEREST EXPENSES

You've got to keep in mind that 99 percent of these types of business sales are asset sales, not stock sales. This means that loans and the interest on them do not carry forward to the new owner.

Therefore, if there is an interest expense on your P&L amounting to $10,000 a year, it is clearly an add-back and an expense that does not carry forward to the new owner of the business.

Chapter 11: Level One Add Backs Example

Total Net Income	6,190	5,379	16,228	4,487	11,280	-856	11,611	28,695	21,799	28,770	53,184	110,975	297,742
Add Backs													
Owner Payroll	4,095	4,095	4,095	4,095	4,095	4,095	4,095	4,095	4,095	4,095	4,095	4,095	49,143
Health Insurance (Owner)	493	493	493	493	493	493	493	493	493	493	493	493	5,916
Amortization	0	0	0	2,137	0	0	0	0	0	0	0	0	2,137
Depreciation	0	0	0	0	0	0	0	0	0	0	0	326	326
Charitable Contributions	0	0	0	300	0	0	0	300	0	0	0	300	900
Interest Expense	317	326	362	301	299	276	272	259	248	201	189	156	3,206
Level 2s...													
Level 2s...													
Level 3s...													
Level 3s...													
Total Add Backs	4,905	4,914	4,950	7,326	4,887	4,864	4,860	5,147	4,836	4,789	4,777	5,370	61,628
Total SDE	11,095	10,293	21,178	11,813	16,168	4,008	16,472	33,843	26,636	33,559	57,961	116,345	359,370

It is critically important to note that it is rare that I'll see six rows of add-backs per level. The example pictured is for demonstration purposes only.

LEVEL TWO ADD-BACKS: THE NOT-SO-OBVIOUS

Any non-recurring expense *during the trailing twelve months* becomes an add-back. You won't always account for every single purchase the business has ever made though—the logo design and legal fees that happened when you launched the business won't factor in and impact your trailing twelve months SDE. But depending on the business age and complexity of the P&L, it may make sense to capture these add-backs going back to inception. If you don't, then SDE as a percent of total revenue may reflect an inaccurate growth in the trailing twelve months.

Some of these Level 2 add-backs could be considered fairly obvious. Yet with what little accounting education and hands-on EXITpreneur experience the vast number of entrepreneurs have, I find these to be not-so-obvious way too many times.

Here are the six subcategories of Level 2:

1. Owner Payroll Tax Expense and Estimated Income Taxes

2. Trademarks, Copyrights, Patents, Logo Design

3. Legal Expenses

4. New Bookkeeper

5. Equipment Purchases

6. Personal Miscellaneous

OWNER PAYROLL TAX EXPENSE AND ESTIMATED INCOME TAXES

It's easy to forget that when you put yourself on salary, your LLC or corporation pays a percentage of that salary in payroll taxes (not income) that go toward social security, etc. Be sure to do the math and create an add-back line for these taxes your company paid on top of your own salary.

You may think it doesn't add up, but here's a sample tax expense pulled from a quarterly statement in the state of North Carolina:

The quarterly payroll amount is just under $43,000, and quarterly Total Employer Taxes are $3,264. Multiply this amount times four to annualize it and you get $13,056. Multiply that times your list price multiple of, say, three, and you get $39,168. If you pay attention to add-backs and this is your payroll, you've just made sure you didn't lose $39,168 in value when you listed and sold your business.

I'll often see estimated income taxes in a P&L. As a self-employed person you are required to pay estimated income taxes on a quarterly basis. If you happen to do this through your business because that is where your money is, then it is clearly an add-back. The alternative is to take a distribution, which does not show up on the P&L, and pay the estimated income tax through your personal account.

TRADEMARKS, COPYRIGHTS, PATENTS, LOGO DESIGN, ETC.

The vast majority of these expenses occur early on in a business's life cycle. But on the off chance they are on the books for the twelve months prior to selling, they are an add-back. These are generally one-time expenses that do not recur, and therefore will not be an expense a new owner will incur.

If they are sizable in value and your business is only twenty-four to thirty-six months old, it may make sense to still put older add-backs in the add-back schedule to properly reflect SDE growth or decline as a percent of total revenue on a year-over-year basis.

LEGAL EXPENSES (LAWSUITS, ENFORCEMENT LETTERS, INCORPORATION DOCS)

I've been self-employed since 1997 and have never been sued. If I were selling my business and had an expense on the books for a "lawsuit" in the twelve months prior to selling, it's not a leap of faith to argue this expense would not recur annually. The same goes for a draft of a patent enforcement letter, incorporation documents, and one-time legal expenses that occur because you are preparing your business for sale.

Now, if there were a lawsuit just prior to selling, you *should* expect to be grilled about why it happened, the outcome, and the risk of it occurring again under new ownership. This is part of the Risk Pillar and will be a big concern for buyers. Don't hide it—they'll find out. Get ugly fast and be honest and open. It's the best way to build trust.

NEW BOOKKEEPER SETTING UP BOOKS IN ARREARS

Have I mentioned that you need to have good P&Ls to get max value for your business? At least a dozen times at this point, so I'll stop here. For now. But if you are like most of us entrepreneurs, you bootstrapped an idea into a successful business. You hate accounting and roughly know your numbers, so you focus on marketing instead of your P&L, balance sheet, or cash flow statement. I understand. I did it too.

But now I know, after reviewing thousands of P&Ls for online businesses, and only listing and selling a fraction of them, that good financials are your ticket to a potential successful exit. They get you in a room with legitimate buyers. Once you are in the room, everything else we're talking about in this book matters. If you want "in the room" in the first place, you'll need a P&L with a monthly view exported to Excel.

I know, I know—"But my CPA only does my books quarterly." Fire your CPA. You should be reviewing your P&Ls monthly at a minimum, and your buyers will do the same. This *is* the online business world after all. As I type this, Mark Zuckerberg just lost $7 billion in net worth in the last two weeks when marketers expressed unease with how Facebook handles misinformation and hate speech. My point is this is the online world and things can change overnight—so clean books with monthly views are critical to a great successful exit.

If you are like I once was and you need to hire a bookkeeper to pull data into QBO or Xero from prior years, this is a one-time expense and absolutely an add-back. The cost of doing this will vary depending on the size and scope of the project, but that cost will not carry forward annually. The monthly cost to maintain the books properly will carry forward, but the one-time expense to get everything cleaned up well in advance of a sale does not.

EQUIPMENT PURCHASES (VIDEO EQUIPMENT, PERSONAL COMPUTERS, ETC.)

In the year prior to selling, a client and her business partner bought some video equipment to film weekly Facebook live events. Because the equipment purchase is not an annual expense, it was considered an add-back. Some could argue that the equipment will become outdated and should only be a partial add-back. And they could be right. With tech evolving so quickly, this could happen. It could also be true that your new Pixel, iPhone, or Galaxy is so good you won't need any new equipment.

Within most small business P&Ls, there always seems to be a bump in Office Expenses in the fourth quarter. This is often because owners are buying equipment they know they need, and want to also get that tax deduction before the year's end. More often than not these laptops and Macs and PCs do not transfer in a sale. Data is no longer stored on them—it's in the cloud. There are no offices with lots of staff with PCs that stay as people come and go. The data transfers in a sale, but the equipment does not—therefore, it is an add-back.

PERSONAL MEALS AND ENTERTAINMENT, TRAVEL, VEHICLES, MOBILE PHONES, HOME OFFICE RENT AND UTILITIES

Let's assume your mobile phone is used for both personal and business calls. Does that mean it is only a partial add-back? No. You've got to remember that we're only talking about online businesses being sold here. Anyone buying an online business already has a mobile phone, so it's not an additional expense or one that will carry forward. And let's face it, if they don't own a mobile phone, they should not be buying an online business.

I am in no way endorsing or encouraging you to entirely write off personal meals and entertainment as a business expense. But the reality is that it happens. Especially with online businesses that are operated from home that require little to no meetings outside of Zoom or Skype calls. Your CPA will make the proper adjustments on your tax returns, but this is rarely reflected in your P&Ls.

If you are writing off personal meals and entertainment as a business expense for a partial tax deduction, you could be losing much more in the sale of your business if you cannot distinguish personal meals from business ones in your P&L. Most buyers accept these add-backs without question though. A glance at your P&L can easily show that you attended no conferences when the expense occurred that would have required such an expense.

The same goes for travel and vehicle expenses. The first word in this add-back subcategory is "personal." So if it's a personal expense that you run through the business as a write-off, it's an add-back. The challenge is finding these in a complex P&L. Not to mention the potential issues you may incur if you are ever audited!

Home office expenses and associated utilities are certainly an add-back. How much you write off depends on the percentage your home office square footage is of your entire home. This expense does not carry forward either, even though a new owner may choose to do the same with their home office rent.

Some buyers may suggest they need to have an office outside the home, and therefore this is an expense they'll incur. And they are right! When listing a business for sale we cannot account for every possible buying scenario, so we have to make certain assumptions. If a buyer has a specific case where they may incur an expense due to their location, living arrangement, or family, they can work that into their offer using math and logic.

Chapter 11: Level Two Add Backs Example

Total Net Income	6,190	5,379	16,228	4,487	11,280	-856	11,611	28,695	21,799	28,770	53,184	110,975	297,742
Add Backs													
Level 1s...													
Level 1s...													
Owner Payroll Taxes (not income)	311	311	311	311	311	311	311	311	311	311	311	311	3,730
Design Patent (for new SKU)	0	0	0	0	0	6,250	0	0	0	0	0	0	6,250
Legal (buying out partner)	3,346	0	0	0	0	0	0	0	0	0	0	0	3,346
Bookkeeping (in arrears)	0	1,700	500	0	0	0	0	0	0	0	0	0	2,200
Office Supplies (laptop)	0	0	0	0	0	2,300	0	0	0	0	0	0	2,300
Total Travel (Personal)	56	19	1,632	213	22	0	0	79	82	0	1,231	561	3,895
Level 3s...													
Level 3s...													
Total Add Backs	3,713	2,030	2,443	524	333	8,861	311	390	393	311	1,542	872	21,721
Total SDE	9,903	7,409	18,671	5,010	11,613	8,005	11,922	29,085	22,192	29,081	54,726	111,847	319,464

Repeat #2: It is critically important to note that it is rare that I'll see all six rows of add-backs per level. The above is for demonstration purposes only.

> **HOW FAR BACK SHOULD MY FINANCIALS GO?**
>
> A multiple is applied to the trailing twelve months, but that's not all you need to have in place. Ideally, two to three years at the very least are needed (assuming your business is at least that old) in order to tell the full story of the business. A bookkeeper might charge $100–$200 a month for each month that they have to input to QBO if you have not done it to date. The good news is it's a one-time expense that doesn't carry forward, which means it becomes an add-back.

LEVEL THREE ADD-BACKS: DIG DEEP AND PAY ATTENTION
VARIABLE AND PARTIAL ADD-BACKS

Let's play a game: You rebuild your website and file for a trademark in 2021. You plan to list your business in 2022, so the trademark would absolutely be an add-back. That's a given. But what about the website?

An *annual* website redesign would not be an add-back. If you don't do it annually, that doesn't make it an automatic add-back. We might look at how often you do a redesign though. Maybe your profit and loss shows us that you've redesigned your website entirely every four years at an expense of $10,000 per year. That amount isn't going to recur next year, but since it will in four years, 75 percent of it would become an add-back within the trailing twelve months of when you list your business for sale.

What's the math on that error if your business lists and sells at 3.2x? By rushing through add-backs or working with an inexperienced Advisor, you might lose $24,000 ($7,500 × 3.2).

This is where so many people get tripped up. They treat an add-back schedule like a checklist that gets them the rest of the way to a multiple. As an entrepreneur, Advisor, Broker, mentor, and friend to online business owners, it's incredibly frustrating to know just how much detail should go into this step but that just gets missed.

Level one and two add-back sections are relatively common-sensical, right? Now that you know what they are, light bulbs go on and you think, "Easy! I've got this!" But now comes the tough part.

Be prepared to review this section several times, as most people don't get it on the first or second read.

Level 3 add-backs are the most often missed add-backs, where sellers leave tens to hundreds of thousands of dollars on the table at closing. Great for buyers seeking instant equity. Bad for you, the seller who has risked everything to get where you are today. When we see sellers listing their own business for sale and not doing an add-back schedule, we call it an "ignorance discount"—and buyers love ignorance discounts!

None of the six below add-backs will jump out to you or most first-time sellers instantly. But they all are black and white mathematical and logical add-backs that have been accepted by buyers in hundreds of millions of dollars in transactions. They are 100 percent real and 100 percent necessary to understand.

Finally, the subcategories of Level 3 add-backs:

1. Website Redesign

2. Masterminds

3. Cash Back Credit Card Money or Converted Rewards

4. Overpaid Relatives or Bookkeepers

5. Reduced COGS in Trailing Twelve Months (TTM)

6. Reduced Third-Party Fees or Packaging Costs in TTM

WEBSITE REDESIGN

The vast majority of online businesses do not redesign their websites annually, so a full or partial add-back should be in place if you just did one and are selling in the next twelve months. How partial the add-back is will depend on your business history. If this is the second redesign in four years, you can add back 50 percent of the cost. If you have not done it in five years, it might make sense to seek a 100 percent add-back. Much will depend on your niche—and, yes, math and logic.

Website support monthly expenses are not add-backs. We're strictly talking about redesign projects that do not recur annually.

MASTERMINDS (AND RELATED TRAVEL EXPENSES)

But these are business expenses, right? Yes, they are—but the membership to a mastermind does not carry forward in a sale. Nor do the travel expenses or extra few days on each end of the meetup that you and your spouse spend exploring the area. If the new owner of a business is already a member of a master-mind, or chooses to apply and join the same or a new one, that's on them. It's not a required expense, and it does not automatically carry forward.

The two obvious exceptions to this rule are:

1. When you attend these meetups and you take your Chief Marketing Officer (CMO) with you, not your spouse. When any employees attend, it is an expense that does not get added back.
2. If your business model requires attendance in order to gain exposure and clients. An example would be if a SaaS company sponsors an event where the attendees may use the product in their day-to-day business. This is not an add-back, as it is considered part of the marketing for the SaaS business.

There are differences between "mastermind meetups" and traditional events, sometimes called trade shows. The Prosper Show, for instance, is an annual event in Las Vegas geared towards entrepreneurs doing much of their business on Amazon. At this event, there are expert speakers sharing their wisdom, and lots of vendors with booths answering questions from attendees and attempting to gain them as clients. These vendors cannot add back this expense, even though the entrepreneurs attending may be able to. Some may argue most entrepreneurs do this and that it is not an add-back, and depending on the circumstances they *may* be right. In this situation, your Advisor/Broker will need to know much more about your business model and how expenses may carry forward. With that knowledge, the best decision can be made to instill the most confidence in potential buyers.

CASH BACK CREDIT CARD MONEY OR CONVERTED REWARDS

If you spend $200,000 a month on advertising, services, packaging, etc., and are not using any kind of cash back or rewards card, you are losing money and losing value in your business.

Here's how:

- $200,000 × 1 percent = $2,000
- $2,000 × 12 months = $24,000 (this is real cash not put in your pocket annually)
- $24,000 × a 4x multiple = $96,000 NOT added to the list price of your business

Is this fuzzy math? Heck no! Cash back money is simply a discount on your advertising or general expense budget. That discount belongs to you in the form of cash back monies or reward points. It's a legitimate flow of money to your bank account. A clear "owner benefit."

Most entrepreneurs think because they have those monies deposited to their personal account versus their business, it's a slippery or tricky form of "tax mitigation" and not something to be shared. According to many CPAs though, the IRS has not figured out how to tax cash back money and considers it a discount, and therefore it's not taxable as income anyway.

Ignoring cash back money in the add-back schedule costs entrepreneurs hundreds of thousands annually. Especially those who sell direct to individuals or holding companies. They think they are saving money by not using an experienced Advisor or Broker, when the reality is they are undervaluing their business because they are miscalculating Seller's Discretionary Earnings (SDE) to begin with.

Not everyone goes with the cash back option, though. Reward cards that offer a multiple of points for every dollar spent have tremendous appeal, especially for those who love to travel. The AMEX Gold Card offers 4x the points for every dollar spent on advertising (with limits). This is much more appealing to travelers than 1 percent cash back because they get much more bang for their buck with travel, hotels, etc.

If you have chosen to get reward points instead of cash back and you want to sell, you can still use logic and math to convert them to dollars. Let's continue with the AMEX example. AMEX will convert reward points to dollars at a ratio of 1 percent. Therefore, if you have accumulated one million points, you have the equivalent of $10,000.

It's important to track when you gained those points, though. You cannot add back a lump sum of the $10,000 if they were earned over a three-year period. Remember, your listing multiple is a multiple of the trailing twelve months (TTM). So adding back a lump sum of $10,000 that was gained over a thirty-six-month period would over-inflate the value of your business.

The correct way of doing this is to convert the reward points to a dollar value for each month they were gained, and then put each of those monthly values in the add-back schedule. Odds are that no two months will be the same and that the total for the last twelve months will be roughly $3,333 if advertising expenses are steady. Now you have just gained $3,333 × whatever your multiple is—although "gained" is likely not the right word. What you've done is show the true earnings of the business. Then, and only then, can we apply the multiple to those earnings.

Some sellers will argue (incorrectly) that because they used reward points to buy a first class $10,000 international flight for just $500, that they should get the $10,000 as an add-back. Or $9,500 if we're doing our math correctly. This is simply not the case. That international first-class ticket is variable, and it was purchased using points that are worth much more than dollars alone. It's fuzzy math at best. Just trying to explain it here is confusing. It does not compute or pass the math and logic test.

The bottom line is if you take reward points instead of dollars, you'll get to use the credit card's own terms to convert those points into dollars (only in the exported P&L—not in QBO, Xero, or the card account itself) on a monthly basis in the add-back schedule. Choosing a cash back card or a rewards card is up to you and how you live, travel, etc. Either way, it's an owner benefit and should be reflected in the add-back schedule and accounted for in the overall value of the business.

OVERPAID RELATIVES OR BOOKKEEPERS

I worked with a client who was doing $10 million in annual revenue and employed a bookkeeper for $24,000 a year. The bookkeeper was young and inexperienced, and offered nothing more than pulling data into QBO and reconciling accounts. He also did much of it wrong.

My advice to that business owner was to interview professional e-commerce bookkeeping firms and consider outsourcing this work. The goal was to first get the data input correctly, and on a timely basis. The second goal was to save money and increase the value of the business.

A year later, the business was sold. Six months prior to selling, the in-house bookkeeper was let go, and an outsourced professional was hired to do a better job at half the cost. The annual savings was $12,000. The switch occurred six months prior to listing the business for sale, so the TTM savings that would carry forward was $6,000. At a 4x multiple, that increased the list price of the business by $24,000.

I am not advising you to start firing people and outsourcing to boost the value of your business. Sometimes it is the right thing to do, sometimes not. But analyzing your overhead when it comes to staff is an important part of running a business with an eventual exit in mind.

OUTSOURCING IS NOT FOR EVERYONE

Bill D'Alessandro, the owner of Elements Brands in Charlotte, used to live the digital nomad life. He looks back on those days and loves his current mindset and business model instead.

Bill believes hiring employees versus VAs brings you much more value from those employees. And that the extra cost is more than made up for with the efficiencies, work output, ideas, and loyalty you get from those employees. When you hear him speak about it, it's hard to argue against him. His business model is not a typical "lifestyle" business. But he argues that when he's on vacation now, he can truly unplug. When he was a digital nomad he may have worked fewer hours, and often from a foreign country, but truly unplugging never really happened.

REDUCED COGS IN TRAILING TWELVE MONTHS (TTM)

If your cost of goods sold went up three months ago by $1.00 a unit, and you sell 500 units a month, you are $500 a month less profitable. If you are under LOI and your buyer says, "Wait, we need to adjust your SDE by $500 a month for the nine months prior to the COGS increase," they would be correct. In effect, your SDE would be adjusted down by $500 × 9 months, or $4,500.

The exact opposite is true as well.

I sold a business recently where the COGS on one SKU went down by $1.80 per unit three months prior to listing the business for sale. This is an expense of $1.80 × the number of units sold that does not carry forward to the new owner of the business. Using math and logic, we pulled data on the number of units sold per month in the nine months prior to the cost reduction, and multiplied that figure to get the cost savings per month. This is what it looks like as part of the add-back schedule.

Chapter 11: SKU Example

	Units Sold	Savings (x $1.80)
Jan	966	$1,739
Feb	2,149	$3,868
Mar	1,056	$1,901
Apr	1,108	$1,994
May	980	$1,764
Jun	2,315	$4,167
Jul	3,646	$6,563
Aug	1,116	$2,009
Sep	743	$1,337
Oct	0	$0
Nov	0	$0
Dec	0	$0
Total	**14,079**	**$25,342**

In this example, if the business is listed for sale at a 3.3 multiple of SDE, digging deep on costs that do not carry forward results in an adjustment to SDE by $83,629. When I consult with entrepreneurs preparing to sell their business and they allow me to dig deep enough into their business, this type of knowledge is mind-blowing.

REDUCED THIRD-PARTY FEES OR PACKAGING COSTS IN TTM

If you are like me, odds are that you bootstrapped your first business. Meaning we hustled, pulled together some cash and an idea or product, and just got the ball rolling. Over time, we learned more about efficiencies and started outsourcing to

VAs, stopped shipping by air, and maybe even redesigned our packaging to weigh less and take up less physical space. There are a million other ideas that have been implemented to reduce costs long after the business was first launched.

If any of these ideas were implemented in the twelve months prior to listing the business for sale, much like a reduction in COGS, these are expenses that do not carry forward and are therefore add-backs.

If you are aware of specific cost-saving areas but have not found the time to implement them, I'd suggest doing a little math. It could be the end result is not worth the effort. Or if the math results in an add-back like the COGS reduction example above, you might allot some time to tackle that as your next project, knowing what it does to the overall value of your business.

Chapter 11: Level Three Add Backs Example

Total Net Income	6,190	5,379	16,228	4,487	11,280	-856	11,611	28,695	21,799	28,770	53,184	110,975	297,742
Add Backs													
Level 1s...													
Level 1s...													
Level 2s...													
Level 2s...													
Website Redesign	0	0	0	0	7,500	0	0	0	0	0	0	0	7,500
Mastermind Fees	117	117	117	117	117	117	117	117	117	117	117	117	1,404
Cash-Back Money	697	721	881	880	1,295	1,459	922	889	994	1,012	1,142	1,196	12,088
Replaced Bookkeeper	2,000	2,000	2,000	2,000	2,000	2,000	0	0	0	0	0	0	12,000
New Bookkeeping Firm	-500	-500	-500	-500	-500	-500	0	0	0	0	0	0	-3,000
COGS reduction in TTM	1,739	3,868	1,901	1,994	1,764	4,167	6,563	2,009	1,337	0	0	0	25,342
Reduced Pick/Pack Fees with new packaging	122	168	119	227	354	635	0	0	0	0	0	0	1,625
Total Add Backs	4,175	6,374	4,518	4,718	12,530	7,878	7,602	3,015	2,448	1,129	1,259	1,313	56,959
Total SDE	10,365	11,753	20,746	9,205	23,810	7,022	19,213	31,710	24,248	29,899	54,443	112,288	354,701

Repeat for the third time: It is critically important to note that it is rare that I'll see all six rows of add-backs per level. The above is for demonstration purposes only.

Note that when you make an adjustment such as the add-back for the "replaced Bookkeeper," you also have to make a negative adjustment for the new expense. In this case it was the carry-forward costs of the new bookkeeping firm at $500 per month. In the months where there are no adjustments for this and the replaced employee bookkeeper, nothing needs to be done because these are already properly reflected in the P&Ls.

ADD-BACK SUMMARY

The Three Levels of Add-Backs and six points below each level do not capture every single add-back that is out there. Every business is unique and should be looked at individually. The add-backs above should cover most situations, but you've got to dig deep, ask questions, and have multiple conversations to capture the true Seller's Discretionary Earnings.

Now let's look at an example of the monetary impact of all of the add-backs combined on your SDE.

Chapter 11: All Add Backs Combined

Total Net Income	6,190	5,379	16,228	4,487	11,280	-856	11,611	28,695	21,799	28,770	53,184	110,975	297,742
Add Backs													
Owner Payroll	4,095	4,095	4,095	4,095	4,095	4,095	4,095	4,095	4,095	4,095	4,095	4,095	49,143
Health Insurance (Owner)	493	493	493	493	493	493	493	493	493	493	493	493	5,916
Amortization	0	0	0	2,137	0	0	0	0	0	0	0	0	2,137
Depreciation	0	0	0	0	0	0	0	0	0	0	0	326	326
Charitable Contributions	0	0	0	300	0	0	0	300	0	0	0	300	900
Interest Expense	317	326	362	301	299	276	272	259	248	201	189	156	3,206
Owner Payroll Taxes (not income)	311	311	311	311	311	311	311	311	311	311	311	311	3,730
Design Patent (for new SKU)	0	0	0	0	0	6,250	0	0	0	0	0	0	6,250
Legal (buying out partner)	3,346	0	0	0	0	0	0	0	0	0	0	0	3,346
Bookkeeping (in arrears)	0	1,700	500	0	0	0	0	0	0	0	0	0	2,200
Office Supplies (laptop)	0	0	0	0	2,300	0	0	0	0	0	0	0	2,300
Total Travel (Personal)	56	19	1,632	213	22	0	0	79	82	0	1,231	561	3,895
Website Redesign	0	0	0	0	7,500	0	0	0	0	0	0	0	7,500
Mastermind Fees	117	117	117	117	117	117	117	117	117	117	117	117	1,404
Cash-Back Money	697	721	881	880	1,295	1,459	922	889	994	1,012	1,142	1,196	12,088
Replaced Bookkeeper	2,000	2,000	2,000	2,000	2,000	2,000	0	0	0	0	0	0	12,000
New Bookkeeping Firm	-500	-500	-500	-500	-500	-500	0	0	0	0	0	0	-3,000
COGS reduction in TTM	1,739	3,868	1,901	1,994	1,764	4,167	6,563	2,009	1,337	0	0	0	25,342
Reduced Pick/Pack Fees with new packaging	122	168	119	227	354	635	0	0	0	0	0	0	1,625
Total Add Backs	12,793	13,318	11,911	12,568	17,750	21,603	12,773	8,552	7,677	6,229	7,578	7,555	140,308
Total SDE	18,983	18,697	28,139	17,055	29,030	20,747	24,384	37,247	29,477	34,999	60,762	118,530	438,050

Again, keep in mind that I have rarely seen an add-back schedule as long as the one above. I'm simply sharing excessive examples to cover our hypothetical bases. For this example, here's the big math:

Net Income = $297, 742
Without add-backs at a 3.x multiple, the business is valued at $893,226

Add-Backs = $140,308
Total SDE truly equals: $438,050
With add-backs, the true value of the business is:

$3 \times \$438,050 = \$1,314,150$

At a 3x multiple for this business, add-backs captured an additional $420,924 in value. Assuming you read and reread this section multiple times, odds are you like the idea of digging deep and making sure you don't miss any add-backs.

WHAT IS NOT AN ADD-BACK?

Pushing too hard on add-backs erodes trust, and trust is one of the most critical factors when selling your business. Making sure erroneous add-backs don't make it to the add-back schedule is just as important as getting the right ones on there.

Failed advertising campaigns are a common culprit. The new owner is going to test ads on a recurring basis just like you have, and it's not always going to work out. This is not an add-back situation—it's just a normal part of doing business.

Of course, there are exceptions. I'm working with a company

that gave an agency their advertising budget plus a one-time $5,000 fee. The advertising budget is still an expense, but the one-time fee can be considered an add-back.

The difference you're looking for is whether the ad expense was part of normal experimentation or an abnormal, one-off expense.

Another common add-back attempt falls around running out of inventory. Almost any growing e-commerce business is likely to run out of stock now and then. It's part of the game, and that alone rules it out of the add-back schedule. But there's another piece to it too—the math and logic around how much revenue is actually lost in those cases, including third-party platform fees and such, is fuzzy at best. If you can't draw a clear line with math and logic to your add-back, it isn't one.

We've touched on the second owner's salary or salary above forty hours a week, as well as fired staff, but certain types of firings are not add-backs. For example, say you have a critical employee who has been with you for years. You decide to sell your business quickly, and toward the end decide that this person is paid too much. You fire them and take on the work yourself, scrambling to get as much of it done as possible just to improve the bottom line.

That's not an add-back. It's a ploy to artificially boost your SDE. Not only is it unethical, but it won't work. A seasoned Advisor will catch it fast, and then if your buyer hires a due diligence firm such as Centurica (experts—look them up), it will be discovered in due diligence and your deal will fall apart.

Any cost cutting just to increase your value will be obvious, and will erode trust between you and your buyer. If they don't catch it until due diligence, the deal could wind up renegotiated or it could fall apart completely.

Don't manufacture add-backs to maximize your earnings. Use them to paint the most complete picture of your business. Done right, add-backs will shape an accurate valuation and build trust for the buyer, and that is much more likely to lead to maximum value than any tricks or shifted numbers that might tempt you or an aggressive Broker.

TIME OUT

- You've heard people say they sold for a 3x multiple. Good for them! But did they calculate their SDE correctly? "A multiple of what" is a simple question to ask, then ask about cash back money or COGS changes in the TTM to get the full picture and learn if they undersold their business or got the SDE right.

- Don't forget about inventory. If the business above is selling physical products, did that 3x multiple include or exclude the total value of the landed COGS?

- If light bulbs are rapidly turning on in your mind about all of your add-backs, good! Start to track them and make sure that you get the true value of your business as you prepare and plan to sell. For a detailed list of possible add-backs that goes beyond the eighteen examples above, visit EXITpreneur.io/Resources.

- Don't rush. Not digging deep can cost you tens of thousands of dollars in value when you exit. Take your time, educate yourself, learn, train, prepare, and exit with confidence that you are getting maximum value.

CHAPTER 12

VALUATION MULTIPLES

Remember thinking that the valuation of a business is "just" the net income, plus add-backs, times the multiple? It has taken us eleven chapters to fully understand how income and add-backs are calculated, as well as external factors that can sway the value way up or way down. It's taken us the same eleven chapters to understand why we don't go straight for the multiple, but instead start with the question: *multiple of what*?

Now we can spend a brief moment answering your initial question, "What is my multiple?"

Before we look at some general things to consider, I have to offer one more significant disclaimer: no two businesses are alike. You might have a content site doing $500,000 in SDE, but that doesn't mean you can point to a chart and expect an exact multiple to be accurate. All of the nuances of the Four Pillars and Key Metrics apply—every time.

In other words, if all you're doing is flipping to this chapter to get the one answer you're looking for, you've wasted your time and money with this book. If you're ready to do the work necessary to become an EXITpreneur, read the whole enchilada and start to apply it to your business.

VALUE RANGES BY NICHE

We're going to limit the "niches" to three—with some caveats and notes for each to keep things simple. The niches are:

- Physical products
- Content
- SaaS

As a reminder: without accurate SDE, your multiple means absolutely nothing.

PHYSICAL PRODUCT VALUATION MULTIPLE RANGES

Let's start with product-based e-commerce businesses. With the advent of third-party platforms such as Amazon, eBay, Walmart, and so on, we have to separate out e-commerce businesses that sell the majority of their products via their own website versus a majority on a third-party platform. Why? With third-party platforms there are many advantages—like that's where most people shop and buy. But the big disadvantage is you don't "own" the customer. You don't get full access to their online contact information to market them additional products and services. You cannot contact them when you are launching new SKUs. You cannot do many things directly with and for them, and this decreases the value of a majority third-party platform e-commerce business when compared to a business selling most products on their own website.

Chapter 12: Channel Valuation Gap

	Your Own Website	Third-party Platform
Revenue & SDE Growth	Yes	Yes
Category Leadership	Yes	Yes
Strong Margins	Yes	Yes
Owns Customer Data	Yes	No
Multi-Channel Revenues	Yes	No
Multiple Ranges	1–10x	1–6x

A 1–2x multiple would indicate the business is high risk.

A 5–6x multiple would be exceptional in all areas and have SDE north of $1 million.

A 7–10x multiple would be larger and have high recurring revenues and stronger growth ahead.

The above multiple ranges are very broad—and this is intentional. Below we'll narrow it down a bit more. Businesses with downward trends may list for lower multiples than those below.

Chapter 12: Channel Valuation Gap (cont'd)

SDE	Your Own Website	Third-party Platform
< $100,000	3–4x	2–3x
$100,000–$500,000	3–5x	2–3.5x
$500,000–$1,000,000	4–6x	3–5x
>$1,000,000	6+	4+

At the end of the transaction, the dollar value to you is the same with or without inventory added to the list price. And you'll remember the amount you sold the business for, not your multiple.

In the above multiple ranges, things are not as simple as "the book says I get a 4+ multiple if my SDE is above $1 million." If it were that simple you would not need Advisors to make sure you are not over- or under-valuing your business. Remember the "What Buyers Want" section in Chapter 4 and the Four Pillars? SDE is not the end-all deciding factor to what multiple is applied to your business.

WHOLESALERS

With regard to physical product businesses, they are not all created equal. If you are a wholesaler, meaning you sell other people's products online on their behalf, your multiple ranges will likely be lower. These businesses are not as defensible or expandable when compared to owning your own brand, where how far you take it is up to you and your limitations.

If you are an online wholesaler the best way to increase your business's value is to think about your buyer and the defensibility of your business. This may mean exclusive contracts, multiple brands, and lots of diversification to offset risk. Go back to Chapter 4 and review the Risk Pillar and implement what you need to in order to offset risk to your buyers, and you'll find your multiple rise when you eventually exit.

CONTENT SITE VALUATION MULTIPLE RANGES

I love the content business model. It requires patience though, and you will not "get rich" quickly. When I built my physical product e-commerce business, my developer told me to "write good quality content that delivers what your audience wants and Google will reward you." He was right. It's not as simple as that of course, but it worked. I had the luxury of spending plenty of money on PPC to drive traffic and convert visitors to paying customers who bought products, so it was not a pure content play.

To date, the largest business I have ever sold was a content site. The organic traffic was continually climbing, revenue growth was 300 percent YOY, and site visitors were hungry for the topic and visited multiple times a day.

In many ways content sites are easier to operate and can generate more predictable cash flows than physical product businesses. Because of this they can be easier to sell and often sell for higher multiples. Much depends on the niche, age, and revenue model though. While the multiples below look exactly like the physical products sold on your own website above, the reality is that content sites lean a bit more toward the higher end of the ranges much more often.

Chapter 12: Content Site Valuation Multiple Ranges

SDE	Multiples
< $100,000	3–4x
$100,000–$500,000	3–5x
$500,000–$1,000,000	4–6x
>$1,000,000	6+

I've sold content sites at or below the 3x multiple range due to trends, keyword rankings, etc. I've also sold or been involved in sales that have blown away the 6+ figure above. So much depends on the niche, trends, revenue model, and foundation the business is built on. Overall though, the content business model is a good one that buyers love when the details are right.

SAAS BUSINESS VALUATION RANGES

SaaS businesses are generally valued higher than both content and physical product businesses. There even comes a tipping point where the business may be valued at a multiple of revenues, instead of earnings.

At Quiet Light, we're fortunate enough to have two of the foremost experts on SaaS business valuations on the team. Both Chris Guthrie and David Newell know more about what adds or plummets value for SaaS businesses than anyone else I know. Sure, I have sold and will continue to sell SaaS businesses myself, and I have sold them all as a multiple of SDE in the multiple range as low as 2.5x and as high as 6x. But my knowledge pales in comparison to what David and Chris know.

In fact, David wrote a 13,000-word article (basically a book) for Quiet Light on SaaS valuations and when the multiples flip from a multiple of SDE to a multiple of revenues.

You can read the full article here: https://www.quietlightbrokerage.com/guide/build-value-and-sell-a-saas-business.

Or do a Google search for "quiet light SaaS 6 7 or 8 figures" and the article will land on the top of the page.

Here are a few excerpts from David's article that will shed some light on SaaS valuations.

"SaaS valuation starts out with SDE but then changes to Revenue after a certain threshold. This causes a lot of confusion in the SaaS valuation marketplace. Founders often think their business is worth a lot more (or a lot less) than it's actually worth. Let's look at why this happens, and whether SDE or Revenue applies to your business."

"Bootstrapped SaaS businesses are valued like every other small business, using a multiple of seller's discretionary earnings (SDE). This reflects the relatively small size of the business, the codependency between the owner at this stage, and the yet-to-be proven scalability of the business."

"Early SaaS businesses experience relatively high customer churn (>4 percent per month) and instability in core metrics like LTV, ARPU, CAC. This happens as they try to find product-market-fit, maturity, and scalability. All of this is to be expected. But what it means is that the best proxy for business earnings is its actual current earnings. That means a multiple of the SDE is the most appropriate valuation in this situation."

"Once the business establishes strong product-market-fit, it will scale to the point where more staff are required to replace the owner. Having more customers means more demands and more complexity. This means hiring is needed to help with:

- Customer onboarding to reduce churn
- Removing the owner and installing developers
- Creating a marketing department to grow the business.

This transformation takes the business from a lite-SaaS to a company-SaaS. This propels the business into a different valuation landscape."

"Adding more overhead to the business naturally reduces its profitability, sometimes quite substantially. In this situation, a multiple based on profit no longer makes sense. Instead, the revenue line becomes the basis for valuing the business. That's because revenue is now the best proxy for the future cash flow of the business, assuming it continues to grow.

So why does this only happen with SaaS and not other models?

This is because a growing SaaS business expects future income to take a long time to materialize. That can happen even with robust underlying unit economies. Sales and marketing expenses are recognized upfront, while revenue persists over many years.

This lag makes new customers unprofitable in the short term, even though they clearly will be profitable over their lifetime. If a SaaS business is growing quickly, there are a lot of new, temporarily unprofitable customers making your net income negative. This is true, even if the business stops growing.

This is why revenue is a better indicator of long-term cash flow for a SaaS business compared to net income, or EBITDA. However, a big caveat to this is the importance of revenue growth. This is a hugely important metric for SaaS businesses, more so than any other business model.

In looking at SaaS businesses, buyers must filter between "lite-SaaS" and "company-SaaS" using a few qualitative and quantitative factors. Buyers put your business through "The Four Tests" to evaluate your size, growth, PMF, and team.

Businesses that are considered "company-SaaS" receive a revenue multiple that passes most or all of The Four Tests:

- Annualized Recurring Revenue (ARR): $1M+ (The Size test)
- Revenue Growth (YoY): 40%+ (The Growth test)
- Monthly Churn: <4% (The Product-Market-Fit test)
- Team: Dedicated Customer Success & Development Teams/ Employees (The Key-Man test)

These are not hard-and-fast rules. They can change depending on each situation, but it's important to remember that The Four Tests are general guidelines that many buyers use to evaluate your business. If your SaaS business is a little below $1M ARR, it could well qualify for a revenue multiple, particularly if there is a strong strategic fit for an acquirer (who will value their synergies based on revenue). The best thing to do is speak to an Advisor in the space to establish what makes sense in your situation."

A FINAL WORD ON MULTIPLES

I'd like to eliminate the need for multiples altogether. Can we all agree to do that now and only focus on dollar values? No? I didn't think so. So let's do this instead: Let's accept the fact that multiples are not dollars deposited to our bank accounts. And that when our business sells we get very fuzzy on what the actual multiple was it sold for.

I know this because I've sold my own and hundreds of others for EXITpreneurs like yourself. On the *Quiet Light* Podcast I've even interviewed EXITpreneurs who sold their businesses through our competitors. When we drilled down to the multiple their businesses sold for, not a single one could confidently give me a number. To be fair, neither could anyone else. I remember dollars, so do my clients, and so will you.

CHAPTER 13

FBA ROLL-UPS

YEA OR NAY?

FBA roll-ups are becoming quite common. As of this writing, the top five have raised over a billion dollars to buy up Amazon FBA businesses. For the FBA business owner, the question is—is this good or bad?

If you are not an FBA entrepreneur, don't skip this chapter. While not as common, there are roll-up firms also focused on the SaaS and content niches. And with the clarity and excitement around the FBA roll-up model, the odds are good that investors will fund more SaaS and content roll-ups as well.

THE BASICS

I know many of the founders and execs at the top FBA roll-up firms, and they are good people. They're intelligent, driven, and well-funded. They are also willing to take on a much higher level of risk than a typical lifestyle entrepreneur. It is my firm belief that the value of FBA businesses will climb because of the competition between these roll-up firms and the individual investors.

What do they do? They buy a single FBA business valued at 2–3x SDE and add it to their portfolio, where it instantly becomes worth 10x or more. The math is simple. The logistics, management, and reporting to investors are not.

SHARK TANK

With dozens of roll-up companies competing against each other to buy FBA businesses, it is natural for the multiples to climb. But this only works to your benefit if you take advantage of the competitive environment.

The hit television show *Shark Tank* doesn't have just one shark in it. Imagine pitching your business to just Mr. Wonderful— you get the picture. The same holds true for presenting your business to just one FBA roll-up company.

1. If you present your business for sale to just one FBA roll-up firm, they will feel no pressure to offer you maximum value and a great deal structure.
2. If you present your business for sale to all FBA roll-up firms, they will compete against each other to buy your business and offer you more cash at closing and better terms.
3. If you present your business for sale to all FBA roll-up firms and all individual buyers, they will all compete even more and pay you the best possible price for your business with the absolute best terms it deserves.

And you do deserve the best price and terms. You've worked incredibly hard and taken on a lot of risk to build your business, so it just doesn't make sense to sell to that one roll-up firm that reached out to you, because they are not offering you the best possible price and terms.

Auctioneers don't put a single chair in the auction room. That would be silly, so why would you?

Which do you think will yield the best result?

THE PITCH

"We'll pay you cash, close in thirty days, and save you the cost of using a broker." That's it in a nutshell. What is not mentioned is that they'll often require a couple of months' worth of inventory as "working capital," hold back a portion of the sale (e.g.) as a "stability payment," and also seek an earnout equal to or greater than the holdback.

They don't mention that they don't want you to go to market with your business because they know they'll have to pay more and offer better terms. All of this does not make them bad people. As I said, most of them are very nice, likable, and trustworthy—that's partly how they convinced investors to give them millions. Because of the investor guidelines and goals, they must look out for their best interest and pitch you on why you should sell to them.

On top of all of that, most who sell direct don't fully understand add-backs and properly calculating SDE. Not to mention their books may be on a cash basis instead of accrual, depressing the real SDE and true value of their company.

Now that you've learned all about add-backs, cash vs. accrual, what buyers want, and multiples, spread the word and help ensure that your fellow FBA entrepreneurs exit at the best value and deal structure. Tell them not to get caught up in the hype of selling to a roll-up firm. Tell them they don't "got this." They've worked hard to get where they have—they should present their business for sale to all potential buyers if they want what is best for them and their families.

PART IV

THE BIG WIN

CHAPTER 14

TEAMING UP FOR THE SALE

The valuation process—what we've covered to this point—is simply knowledge. It's not a magic wand that sells your business. It's not a commitment that you'll never be able to back out of. So why don't more entrepreneurs do it? Why are so many people sitting on their biggest asset without knowing what it's worth? I've found the answer is often two-fold: either they think they're too small to engage with an Advisor who can help them, or they think they have to be *ready to sell* before they can reach out.

Don't make that mistake.

It doesn't matter if you're not planning to sell for twelve months, twenty-four months, or more. A current valuation is important to the process, and you need help to get it done right.

What I've given you in this book is enough to be ahead of your peers. It's enough to make you finally believe in your own eventual exit, no matter what that timeline looks like. It's enough to be dangerous—and probably a little better than that. But most importantly, it's enough to launch a good relationship with an Advisor.

Things change. Valuations go up and down. Some of the many nuances and differences between your business and the next will push the value above or below the ranges we've seen in the marketplace. I can't list every possible unique factor for every business here—there's just no replacement for real-life interaction.

With that said, there's a difference in reaching out to an Advisor to sell versus reaching out to an Advisor for a valuation. Up to this point, we've focused heavily on valuation. Since you've read this far, I think we can safely assume you're an EXITpreneur at heart. You're going to sell. You'll get through the pain of this first exit, and then you'll be ready to start all over again, this time with the end in mind.

So let's walk through that part of the process together—what it looks like to engage when it's time to get serious, and what you can expect as you get closer to your own incredible exit.

ENGAGING WITH AN ADVISOR

The right Advisor will have your best interests in mind, not theirs. Sometimes, that looks like them telling you to go away— it's not the right time to sell your business. That's exactly what happened to me when I wanted out. I had taken my radio and TV infomercial-based product 100 percent online in 2005, and then took it through the best and worst of the economy in the coming years. It was awesome and exhausting. By the spring of 2010, I needed and wanted something else.

Selling an online business wasn't common at that point, so it wasn't something I planned for at all. Once it dawned on me that an exit might be possible, I started searching online for

Advisors/Brokers who might help me. I managed to find three of them, and I took the time to talk to each of them multiple times. With two of the three, I could almost feel them standing up, leaning over their speakerphone trying to reach through the lines to get their hooks into me for a commission. They told me what they thought I wanted to hear. They gave me glorious valuation estimates. They made promises that I wasn't sure they could keep.

They weren't trying to help me as much as they were trying to talk me into signing an engagement letter. I hated it.

The third firm was Quiet Light, where I had a pleasant call with Mark Daoust. Mark explained that he'd been in my shoes before. He was an entrepreneur who understood how much I wanted out, but that there was more to it than that. He asked a lot of questions about my business, and while he did give me some general value ranges over the phone, he wouldn't make any promises. A deeper look was required before we could understand what the business was really worth.

Without any kind of engagement letter or commitment, I sent Mark the profit and loss statements exactly the way he asked for them, and we set up another call to review. He went through the whole add-back process, firmed up the Seller's Discretionary Earnings, and pointed out that the improving economy and my improving business showed a stronger trailing twelve months than the comparable months in the previous year. Months nine, ten, eleven, and twelve were weak though, but with each new month, I made more in total revenue and Discretionary Earnings than I had in that comparable month the previous year. Mark said if we waited for a few more months, my overall trailing twelve months of Discretionary Earnings would increase substantially, and so would the value of my business.

He explained that the reality was we could sell my business that day for a certain amount, but if I waited another six months, we could sell it for a fair amount more.

After all that time spent on my valuation, he essentially told me to go away. He was willing to help me the right way at the risk of losing his cut of the deal. Helping me was his first priority, and because of that, there was no one else I could imagine working with.

Mark didn't ask me to sign a contract yet. He just helped me. He gave me the tools and education I needed to make decisions that were best for me and my business. I put that plan together, learned an awful lot in the process, and strengthened the business before reaching back out to list it. The business was listed in the early fall, and it was under contract with a Letter of Intent within three weeks.

I can always tell when someone is truly interested in selling because they won't let us off the phone without us giving them a ballpark number. They want to know what their business is worth because they want to know how close they are to selling. That ballpark figure has to come with a grain of salt, however. It's only based upon the information we have *so far*.

Often, I'll walk a seller through the same education I've given you here, then they'll tell me what their discretionary earnings are, and I'll give them an estimate. Then the full add-back schedule changes things, often significantly. I've seen values jump by as much as $500,000.

It can't be said enough: At this point, you have just enough information to be dangerous. Don't go it alone.

PERSON-TO-PERSON TRANSACTIONS

A mentor once told me, "Joe, it just sounds like you're giving stuff away for free and hoping that you earn their business."

That's exactly it, and it's a model that works.

I share this because I want you to understand my motives. My entire goal is to help you reach your goals. Anything else I might want is secondary and stems from you, in fact, reaching your goals. The best Advisors are here to be helpful, no matter what that looks like for an immediate return. While I can't speak for any other firms, that's our M.O. at Quiet Light.

In one instance, my colleague Brad Wayland hit it off with an entrepreneur at a mastermind so well that he wanted to hire Brad as an additional Advisor to the firm he had already hired. Brad said, "No, we don't do that, but you can talk to me anytime. We'll have lunch, grab dinner—whatever you need. Just pick up the phone and call me."

Brad didn't help with the intention of gaining that person's business. He did it because he's been there before and knows how important it is to have people in your world you can turn to for advice. Brad became that person for this individual, and eventually wound up becoming his Advisor as well. The original deal fell through, and when the entrepreneur set up a new engagement with Brad, they wound up getting offers for nearly twice as much for the business.

Like hiring a real estate agent, you can and should look at their listings and closed transactions. You can ask for referrals, since this is a small industry, and someone in a mastermind or Facebook group will likely know of them. But at the end of the day, this isn't actually real estate. This process is emotional for the seller and, oftentimes, the buyer. The true mark of a reliable Advisor is whether they're going to help you through that emotional process to reach *your* goals—not theirs.

The best Advisors are the ones who've been preparing for the role their entire lives without knowing it. They've built, bought, or run their own online businesses, then sold them. They've had some great successes in life, and they've had some epic failures, and those successes and failures made them better as Advisors.

Find an Advisor who treats you like a person and wants to see you succeed. Find someone who's willing to help you, not someone who needs your business to help them.

GETTING THE TIMING RIGHT

Timing is just as important to consider as value—when you would like to get out, when you can realistically hit that goal, and any seasonal considerations you need to make. You're about to entrust your most valuable asset to a buyer, and how it is presented to the world matters, both for the success and timing of the sale.

I'm often asked about the best time to sell a business, but that's not what timing is actually about. A great business that isn't seasonal in nature will sell any time of year. A business that's *incredibly* seasonal, with 80 percent of the revenue coming through in a couple months of the year, is a different story. If the bulk of your revenue comes in November and December and you think you'll just hold the business, capture all that revenue, and list it for sale in January, you're not thinking about the new owner.

Let's look at the math. Say someone buys a business for $2 million with an SBA loan. If the loan payments are $18,000 a month for ten years, and the new owner bought the business in February, 80 percent of the revenue doesn't kick in until the following November and December. The buyer will lose money for ten months before turning a profit. The loan, cash flow to live on, inventory for the fourth quarter—it would all put the buyer in the red.

In reality, that probably wouldn't happen, because the odds are lower that anyone would buy that business just after a seasonal peak.

When I ran into this scenario with a client a few years ago, I knew it would take an extra sixty to ninety days to close if the buyer had SBA funding, so we backed up our list date from there. We listed in early summer and managed to close in October. Over the next two months, the buyer received 80 percent of the annual revenue, earning funds for the monthly loan payments of $18,000 from January through October.

The funny thing is when you think about other people and what's best for them, it usually ends up being great for you, too.

In another case, the seller had a seasonal hero SKU that produced the vast majority of the revenue in his business in a short window at the end of the year. Not only did most of the revenue come from one SKU, but it also came from one great ad on Facebook.

A year or so before he wanted to sell, I advised him to expand his SKU count and test more ads in order to increase his multiple and overall value, but he thought it was too much work and too much risk. He literally told me the great thing about his business—and what made it more valuable—was that it was so easy to manage with one SKU and one ad. He didn't expand.

He eventually decided on another firm that made big promises and didn't think at all about the buyers. Not only did his business not sell, because no one wanted to buy his highly seasonal business in January, just after the high season, but the revenue trends came down by 50 percent over the previous year because that great performing Facebook ad was disallowed for unexplainable reasons. Sadly, no other ad variations could achieve the same ACOS, and revenue and profits continued to go down dramatically. To my knowledge, his business never sold.

If he had been thinking about the next owner, he would have held the business, de-risked it, and continued to grow it. And with an eventual early fall sale, he could have handed it off just in time for the big rush, and with more SKUs and ads to offset the risk.

Buyers are looking for a return on investment, and they want to make sure that investment is relatively safe and one that will grow. Confidence is built with numbers. Trust is built with decisions you make along the way, that take a buyer's investment into consideration.

I've spoken with thousands of entrepreneurs about exiting their business, but have only gone through with a couple hundred listings. It's not often the seller walking away—it's me educating them on value and timing. And them realizing they've got some work to do before being able to reach their exit goals.

GETTING TO YES (OR NO)

"I know we signed an engagement letter, but I'd love to wait. Can we do that?"

It happens when the seller is reinvigorated and wants to grow the business more. It happens when they learn so much in the process of listing their business for sale that new potential opens up.

My personal answer to that question is that I can't force you to do anything, even when we have signed an engagement letter. What am I going to do—push you toward a deal you don't want until you dig your heels in the ground and the buyer quits anyway? No, we have to have trust. We have to have a good relationship. If you need to walk away from the sale for a while, I'll be here when you're ready again.

I can't speak for other Advisors, however, so check the length and terms of your engagement letter. Ninety days makes sense in my experience. A six- or twelve-month commitment could turn into a mess.

Make sure you feel good about the person you're working with. Someone overpromising and underdelivering is a red flag. Making a decision to sign an engagement letter after one call is iffy. If you do it because you have full confidence in the Advisor's experience and/or they were referred to you, great. If you do it because they dazzle you with charm and big numbers, take a minute and make sure you have a second or third call before signing. Signing an engagement letter is a big commitment; make sure it's right for both of you. Choose somebody you connect with and trust. Someone who's truthful. Someone with a reputation of success in the industry.

If you have multiple Advisors that you like and have bonded with, visit their websites and inquire on a listing or two. You'll have to sign a nondisclosure agreement to review the full details. This should feel like an obvious step, but too few people actually take it. Skimming a website doesn't give you the level of detail that's crucial to the actual sale. The online information provided with a listing is just a teaser. It's the full listing details and the work that goes into them—and instilling confidence in buyers—that separate the good from the great.

Next, try to look at the listing details from a buyer's perspective. Is it an attractive listing? Is the summary well-written and presented properly? Are the financials well-formatted and in the must-have monthly view? Can you download the P&L in Excel and make your own projections? Are they put together in a way that builds trust and instills confidence?

Great Advisors aren't necessarily inspiring or persuasive. That's fine, because you can't talk someone into buying a business anyway. Instead, great Advisors work hard, grind it out, think of their client first, and are helpful people with a great eye for detail.

Similarly, great listings aren't about the Advisor's credentials. They reflect that eye for detail and build trust. They present the information in a way that helps buyers make the best possible decisions—because while it is an emotional process, it's not an emotional decision. Math and logic build trust, and trust sells businesses.

CHAPTER 15

STRUCTURING THE DEAL

"A confused mind always says no."

It's not my quote, and I don't believe it is meant to be insulting. What I believe it means is we, as humans, have a tendency to reactively say "no" to things we're not fully familiar with. This is one of the reasons I rarely ask a client if they are willing to accept a seller note, or earnout. I do fully explain what these terms are and the likelihood an offer from a buyer will include any of these for their business. But rarely do I straight up ask, "Will you accept an earnout?"

Why? Even with a full explanation of what the different deal structures are, my client still doesn't know who the eventual buyer is, and therefore, they are "confused" about the type of person the buyer is and what characteristics they may have when combined with a note, earnout, or equity roll.

If you are a buyer reading this book (good for you), you should not email the listing Broker or Advisor and ask, "Is your client flexible on price and willing to accept a partial earnout?" Hopefully as you are reading this you are thinking *that's not a good approach*, and you'd be right. It does happen though. With every business I list for sale, I get at least one email that asks these types of questions. Generally, they are from people just beginning their search and they are unfamiliar with our process. If the listing Advisor gets an email like this from someone (you) they don't know, the Advisor is ignorant and "confused" as to who you are and what type of buyer you really are. Lots of assumptions come into play at this point, and they are generally not good, or accurate. Mr. or Ms. Buyer, do the hard work in reviewing the full details of the business, ask intelligent questions, and get to know the Advisor and seller before making an offer.

When a buyer likes a listing and requests more information (and they've signed a nondisclosure agreement), they should get an all-encompassing package to review. Your Advisor might call it a Deck, a CIM (confidential information memorandum), or a Business Summary, and it should include everything the buyer needs to know to make a good decision as early as possible. I've seen buyers try to make an offer within an hour of a listing going live, but that's not the offer you want. Odds are they are just trying to pull it off of the market, tie up the listing, and make their real decision later on in due diligence.

Within the first couple months of my tenure as an Advisor for Quiet Light, a client of mine who sold keychains was under contract for around $35,000. But the books were a mess and there was a lot of inventory—as much inventory as the value of the business. However, we managed to pull together enough information to make a presentable package. After a couple of conference calls with an interested party, we went under Letter of Intent (LOI). During due diligence, the buyer, who was from southern California, got on a plane and flew to Minnesota to meet with the seller.[4]

He knew the books were messy and challenging, and that there were a bunch of moving parts that the owner hadn't put together well. We were as clear as we could be in the package, but the business wouldn't have sold without this person hopping on a plane and going to Minnesota to deal with it face to face in due diligence.

Since then, I've sold businesses for owners all over the world, to buyers all over the world. We've spanned Germany, Israel, Canada, Brazil, Ireland, the UK, and the US, and so many more countries. Yet the best way to really instill confidence is for the buyer to "see the whites of your eyes." When the deal is complicated, when there's a lot to sort out, or when you don't share the same first language, body language is important for establishing a rapport that builds trust. In most situations, video conferencing is enough to get it done—and we're all so much more comfortable with this these days. But sometimes, flying into the middle of a Minnesota in the dead of winter is important too.

An offer shouldn't be considered until the buyer has fully digested the profit and loss and client interview, spoken with the Advisor to get their questions answered, and then spoken with you as the seller, preferably on video. Speaking with the owner of the business is so critical, I don't even allow offers to be submitted before that connection is made.

---

4   Side note: It was January, and I tried telling him how many layers he needed to wear. He laughed it off, but later told me how much his ears froze on that trip!

NEGOTIATING A BALANCED PURCHASE PRICE

Regardless of the terms of the transaction, the deal has to be right for both parties. There's no "winner takes all" situation here. If the deal is one-sided, you won't get through to closing. You'll waste your time. You'll go through due diligence only for it all to fall apart.

Consider this cold email that complete strangers often send me (and every other Advisor they can find online):

> I'm looking for a business that is five years old and has at least 15 percent year over year growth. Patents would be ideal, with a barrier to entry on the business, and I would like to buy it with 20 percent down and an 80 percent seller note over the course of five years. I'll pay no more than a 2.2 multiple on earnings.
>
> I'm really excited to get started and look forward to buying something from you really soon.
>
> Many salutations!

These emails go right into the trash where they belong—all the risk would fall on the seller. Nevertheless, sometimes buyers like this still get through to make an offer, and that's when all of their lopsided expectations come to the surface.

Of course, some businesses do deserve a lower multiple with some kind of earnout or seller note, which we'll look at more closely in a minute. If your niche is highly competitive with a very low barrier to entry, and it's a product or service with a big fear of obsolescence, there's too much risk involved to expect a seller to show up with a ton of cash to cover a high multiple.

To avoid one-sided offers going into a Letter of Intent, you have to price the business right. Period. When you price it right, backed by math and logic in the valuation and presentation, you avoid a one-sided offer and can come to an agreement that works for everyone.

CASH OR CREDIT

As mentioned earlier, I generally don't ask my clients whether they're willing to accept an offer outside of cash, because almost every time the answer will be *no*. This changes with deal size, of course. Larger deals can expect some form of payment other than all cash and it's important to communicate that going in.

Cash is familiar and safe and predictable. Instead of pushing my idea of deal structure onto buyers, I put the listing out and let them come forward with offers that work for them. The only way to understand alternatives to cash offers is to know who your buyer is and whether the alternative can be trusted. When you like and trust your buyer and they like and trust you, you're more likely to make something work.

Selling for cash sounds exciting, but like anything else, there are benefits and drawbacks. One potential downside is that cash buyers sometimes get slight discounts, depending on how attractive the business is, how strong the four pillars and metrics are, and how well you built the business with the future buyer in mind.

If you are selling for cash, you may have a variation of the following:

- Cash, plus a Holdback
- Cash, plus a Stability Payment

- Cash, plus a Seller Note
- Cash, plus an Earnout

Now let's review the different types of deal structures below. Some offers may have just one component, while others may have two or three. It all depends on the size and complexity of the business.

SBA DEALS

The head of acquisitions for a well-known holding company, or aggregator, once told me "S, B, and A are my three least favorite letters!" He said this because it means he's competing against buyers that can purchase a business for as little as 10 percent down. This gives them the ability to pay more for the business than he can with his tight investor guidelines.

For you—the business owner—don't be afraid of SBA buyers. In my experience, they are willing to pay a bit more for the business than institutional buyers. Sure, it will take a bit longer to close (cash deals are generally thirty to forty-five days, while SBA deals are up to forty-five to ninety days), but that's just more money in your pocket from owning the business longer.

If SBA funding is involved, a seller note may be required as well. It depends on the size of the business, what the cash flow looks like after closing, and the buyer's own personal cash flow needs. On deals that are sub $1–1.5 million, odds are a seller note won't be required. But every deal is different, so your Advisor will have to get the business reviewed by a qualified and experienced SBA Lender for a professional opinion.

If a seller note is required, you can expect it to be about 10 percent of the total Purchase Price (plus inventory, if any). The terms of the seller note can vary, but the most common I have seen is a five-year note. Yes, you can earn interest on your loan to the buyer, and you should. A reasonable amount commensurate with market rates will do. You are not a credit card company, so don't expect 10–12 percent interest rates. On occasion, we'll see a two-year standby on the note. This means that your payments won't start for twenty-four months. Why the standby? Because the bank is protecting their loan and wants to keep the overhead of your buyer as low as possible in the early days. It's generally backed up with lots of math and logic.

The lender will also provide monies for inventory and working capital as well. They want to see their client succeed and pay back the loan in full.

Generally speaking, to get SBA approval, you'll need at least two years of tax returns. Your Advisor will make the connection with the lender and do all of the work. Most lenders will say they need three years of returns, but I've seen many make it work with two. Either way, this can sometimes be a challenge when a business is listed for sale mid-to-late in the year and has seen exceptional growth within that year. The value of these businesses is calculated mostly off the trailing twelve months (as you now know), but the tax returns are for the previous year(s) and don't reflect what's happening now.

I recently listed a business with incredible growth that was far and above the prior years. The tax returns for the previous three years were available and reviewed by three different lenders. All three came back and offered only partial funding for the business. The business was listed for sale at $3,950,000. The

SBA Lenders were only able to provide $2,200,000 in lending for a qualified buyer.

This is all due to the tax return figures the lenders *must* use when calculating the debt-to-income ratios. While a partial loan may seem like a loss, it's better than nothing at all—which I have seen as well. Sometimes amazing businesses are not SBA eligible because the growth is simply off the charts but that growth isn't reflected in tax returns (yet).

As a seller, I understand that you might prefer a cash buyer versus an SBA one because there could be fewer complexities. But in my years of helping people have incredible exits, I've seen just as many cash deals go sideways as SBA deals. The key is finding the right buyer.

The SBA landscape continually changes. A few years ago, almost every deal required a seller note. That changed to allow for just 10 percent down with no note—and SBA deals spiked. It could change again, so there is no point in saying they *all* work a certain way.

If you are a buyer and want to learn and master the SBA deal process, I'd suggest buying my friend and colleague's book *Buy Then Build*. Walker Deibel did an outstanding job writing his bestseller and helping people understand the value of buying a business versus building one. Buyers can also visit the resource page on our website for a list of trusted SBA Lenders. They are definitely not all created equal, and dealing with the wrong one can be a huge mistake.

As a seller, I'd advise you to leave the preapproval process up to your Advisor/Broker. They have the relationship with the lenders and know which ones to trust and which to avoid.

COMMON DEAL STRUCTURES

When you sell your business, you'll want to know how much money you'll wind up with at closing. Knowing the most common forms of deal structures will help with that learning. If your buyer does not pay all cash or buy the business with an SBA loan—which can be the equivalent of all cash—odds are they'll seek an offer that combines one or more of the following types of deal structures.

SELLER NOTES

Buyers who seek a seller note, more often than not, just want to know that you'll be there for them after closing to help with issues that may arise after the initial training and transition period ends. Since you are not a bank, you should not be expected to hold a sizable percentage of the purchase price or a note for a lengthy period of time.

In my years in this business, I have participated in just two transactions where the seller note was for more than 50 percent of the total purchase price. The first one was for a five-year period, and the second for just twelve months.

In the first one with the five-year note, the seller and buyer bonded quickly and got along like long-lost sisters. They trusted each other and that led to a deal structure that was beneficial for both parties. You might be saying, "How is a five-year note good for the seller?" Because of the trust she had in the buyer, and confidence in the business itself, she felt the note would give her the income stability she was seeking while her investment portfolio matured for another five years.

The second transaction with a 50 percent note was a surprise.

The owner was a mother of four and worked about twenty hours a week on a blog generating $100,000 in annual profits. She started the business part-time and never intended for it to become as big as it did and to have so much responsibility on top of being a mom to four kids under ten.

When the right buyer came forth and offered full price for the business with 50 percent of it on a twelve-month note, she didn't hesitate or even counter. She accepted because she was emotionally exhausted and ready to move on.

The two deals above are the exception, rather than the rule. Again, EXITpreneurs are not banks and should not be counted on to finance someone else's purchase of their business. For most deals where a seller note is involved, I generally see the term for anywhere from twelve to thirty-six months tops. Keep in mind that the larger the transaction, the larger the odds that a seller note or some sort of financing will be needed to make buyers comfortable.

Even though you are not a bank, if you accept a seller note you should earn interest on the note. Matching what the banks charge is a good starting point. Adding a point or two doesn't hurt, but doing the math reveals an extra percent or two on a $100,000 twenty-four-month note doesn't put that much more money in your pocket. Instead of a few extra dollars, I'd focus on seeking security and peace of mind.

If you choose to accept a seller note, consider the five points below to help you sleep better and get paid as well. And as always—hire a good attorney to help you with the written purchase agreement and seller note.

1. Have the note secured personally by the buyer, and with the assets of the business.
2. Keep it short—twelve to thirty-six months is most common.
3. Charge a fair but reasonable interest rate.
4. Have your agreement detail clear steps to be taken if the buyer is in default.
5. Outline the way payments are made and make it easy on both parties. An automated ACH or wire transfer on the same day of the month is best.

If you are selling a product business and have an excess amount of inventory, an even shorter seller note might be in order. For example, if you have $700,000 in landed inventory costs on hand and it represents seven months' worth of inventory, it may be fair and reasonable to offer a three-month seller note on a portion of the inventory. Short notes on inventory are a great negotiating tool for both buyers and sellers.

HOLDBACKS

A Holdback is a tool I have seen used most often with cash deals. It's normally tied to the training and transition period discussed in Chapter 16. Rather than you getting paid 100 percent of the Purchase Price at closing and the buyer "hoping" you'll stick around for answering questions on how to operate the business, a Holdback is put in place as a carrot to make sure you are there for the training and transition period.

If the training and transition period is for up to ninety days, you'll likely see a Holdback that is held in escrow for a ninety-day period, and then released.

The language should be simple and clear and should be part of the LOI and then the asset purchase agreement (APA). It would read something like… "A Holdback equal to 10 percent of the Purchase Price will be held in escrow during a training and transition period of ninety days, and then it will be released." There are no conditions set here. If for some reason you don't comply with the training and transition, then your buyer may get their attorney involved to dispute the Holdback release.

In the hundreds of deals I've been involved with, I have only seen a Holdback not released once. My seller was a single mom living in Texas and the buyer was in Massachusetts. The buyer and his son flew to Texas during due diligence to meet with the seller. They went to her house and spent several hours getting to know her and how she operated the business. They even met her children. They were impressed and excited to move forward with the transaction and buy the business.

The day after closing my seller disappeared, literally. There was a tornado in her hometown and we feared the worst after all calls and emails went unanswered. We contacted the local sheriff, who swung by the house for a visit. According to him there was no visible damage to the home or her area, but she was not at home. After weeks of attempting further contact, the buyer's attorney and the escrow attorney made the decision to not release the Holdback, and the monies reverted back to the buyer. The seller was never heard from again.

I hope the above will not make every buyer nervous! It's happened just once (<1 percent of the time), but highlights the need for the Holdback to raise the comfort level of the buyers. Sellers: your money is in escrow and if the final APA language reads as above, it is simply released assuming you support your buyer during the training and transition period.

Holdbacks can also be used for "true ups." I've seen this on only a handful of deals—and where I did, they were larger and more complex. Some attorneys like to add additional language that holds back a percentage of the Purchase Price for money due to the buyer (or seller) after closing. These monies would be for returns or incidental expenses or income not accounted for in due diligence or nearly impossible to account for in an APA. I do believe there are some legitimate reasons to add this language. But in the hundreds of deals I've done, the "true up" value was only a few hundred to a few thousand to either party—and it was always handled in good faith with a separate ACH, wire, or check after closing.

EARNOUTS

I've often said that earnouts are reserved for a business in trouble—or the opposite: those that are priced on future performance. And this is true for the most part. But as our firm has grown, so have the deal sizes. As we see more transactions in the $10–20 million range, the earnout "ask" happens more and more.

Let me be clear: I don't like earnouts that are based off of EBITDA or SDE. There are too many variables that can be stuffed into the expenses, making the math much more difficult to calculate. Especially if a holding company is buying your business and commingling staff to manage dozens of brands. With that said, I have friends that have made more money on the earnout portion of their sale than the original purchase price, and did it as a percent of EBITDA.

If I were selling a business and had to accept a portion of the sale as an earnout, here's a list of things I would shoot for:

1. Make the payment a percent of total revenue, not Gross Profit, EBITDA, or SDE. It's easy enough to calculate a smaller percentage off the top that is equal to the historical EBITDA figure. Private equity buyers will fight this because it's not standard. But you're risking your business and money on their success and accurate books. Push back and be prepared to walk away if you don't get what you want.

2. Seek monthly payments. Steady payments remove doubt, concern, and the stress of the unknown.

3. If you have a financial cap, structure the earnout so it is "X percent of total revenue up to Y." The Y is your total cap, or payout on the earnout. This type of language is good for both parties. If the business grows rapidly you get paid sooner. If it stagnates your payout will take more time.

4. Like the seller note, keep it as short as possible. You can do the math on a $100,000 earnout cap to get yourself paid out in two years if the business grows at a similar pace under new ownership. If the business does a million a year in revenue and you agree to a 5 percent off the top earnout, you'll get paid $50,000 a year and be paid out in two years.

5. Require access to the data that shows the actual revenues being produced. It's rare that anyone will work hard to create fake reports and pay you less than you deserve, but it's better to be safe than sorry. Tax returns, view-only access to third-party platforms that show revenues, etc., are all sources you can access to verify the revenues they are paying you out on. A good attorney will help with drafting language that will give you access to data while keeping your buyer's information confidential.

While the above is a wish list of what I'd seek if I sold with an earnout, none are guaranteed to happen. And if I really liked and trusted my buyer, I might bend a bit.

STABILITY PAYMENTS

If you run a Google search for "Stability Payments," you won't find much in the way of content that is related to selling or buying an online business. But it is something that more and more holding companies are seeking when buying high-risk online businesses.

The stability payment is a blend of a seller note and earnout. The concept is simple. It generally reads something like this:

> If the revenues of the business are within 90 percent of the trailing twelve-month revenues at closing, you (seller) will be paid a stability payment of X.

The "X" is typically 10 percent of the purchase price of your business, but it can vary.

Let's assume your Stability Payment is $250,000. Here's the problem with the language as written above. If revenues fall short of the 90 percent goal by even just 1/10th of 1 percent, you go from earning $250,000 to zero.

If you choose to accept a Stability Payment, I'd suggest you work some of the points below into your Agreement.

1. Make the 90 percent a sliding scale. If revenues are 90 percent or above, you get paid the $250,000 in full. If the revenues are at or above 85 percent, but less than 90 percent, you get paid $200,000. If they are at or above 80 percent, but less than 85 percent, you get paid $150,000, and so on. This removes the risk of losing everything by being off by 1/10th of 1 percent.
2. Ask for upside on the stability payment. You may not get it,

but it won't hurt to ask for the reverse of the above. If revenues reach 105 percent, you get paid $300,000. If revenues reach 110 percent, your payout is $350,000, and so on. You'll have to make this work for both parties and not create a disincentive for your buyer to grow the business.

3. Retain access to third-party reporting. Holding companies rolling up FBA businesses are most common, and retaining report-only access to the seller account is a simple ask.

4. Add your own stability clause with regard to inventory. If the business does not reach the 90 percent goal because a staffer was bad at their job and didn't order inventory in a timely fashion, you should not be financially punished. Add language that reads something like "If Purchaser runs out of inventory on XYZ SKUs for a period of more than one week in any three-month period, the stability payment will be due in full within thirty days." You'll have to identify XYZ SKUs of course. This will be easier if your business has a hero SKU producing 70 percent of the revenues, versus a well-balanced business with no SKU representing more than 20 percent of total revenues. Any good attorney will add language that the fault of running out of inventory is due to the buyer, not natural events, pandemics, etc.

As with a seller note, hire a good attorney to assist with drafting the language in a way that secures your payments and allows for recourse if you are not paid in full in a timely fashion.

ROLLING EQUITY

"Rolling equity" means you sell a portion of your business for cash, and roll the remaining percentage into a new company set up by your buyer. You don't get cash for the portion rolled, but you get ownership in a new company with the theory that your buyer will grow it to much greater heights than you were able to, therefore increasing your net worth and eventual exit value.

With an equity roll you will clearly have to trust in your buyer's expertise. You'll have to believe they can take the business to much greater heights than you could on your own. You may stay on as a strategic Advisor with your ownership, and odds are they won't need (or want) you for the day-to-day operations of the business.

Sticking with the holding company concept (those buying up FBA businesses), let's contrast the equity roll against the more well-known model of selling everything and moving on.

The majority of holding companies have a goal of buying FBA businesses for a multiple of 2–3x SDE. On top of that they'll seek some working capital (see below), a stability payment, a seller note, and/or an earnout.

It's a steal/deal for them, especially when they roll your business into their portfolio and it becomes instantly valued at 10x versus the 2–3x they just bought it for.[5]

Holding companies that seek equity rolls can provide much more upside to the business owner. Here's how they generally work:

1. They buy 51 percent of your business and roll the remaining 49 percent into a NewCo that you co-own.
2. You stay on as a strategic Advisor. Your role may be new

---

5   In defense of these types of holding companies...there is a lot of risk involved in buying these businesses. Most have hero SKUs and are quite difficult to sell to your typical risk-averse buyer.

product development or something that is more visionary, and does not require the daily grind you've been at for the last few years.

3. They assign a manager to your brand that runs/oversees the day-to-day operations.

4. Because of their size, diversity, etc., your 49 percent instantly becomes valued at 10x SDE, versus the 2–4x it would have sold for to a typical buyer.

You can launch additional brands on your own, or using their resources and an equity split of 50/50. On your own you own 100 percent, grind it out for two to four years taking little out of the company, and sell it for 2–4x SDE. With the holding company, your 50 percent is valued at 10x, but you are not grinding it out—the company uses its resources and brand managers to do the day-to-day work while you strategically advise them and oversee the brand.

The downside to an equity roll is you have little control over when the eventual exit actually occurs. If you wanted "out" you could likely sell your shares, but it's unlikely you'd get the 10x the overall business would get when selling to a private equity buyer.

Let's do some math:

- You're selling your business for 3x SDE of $300,000. The list price is $900,000.
- You sell 51 percent for $459,000 and roll the remaining 49 percent into the NewCo.
- Your 49 percent now represents $147,000 in SDE ($300,000 × 49 percent) and is worth $1,470,000.

The brand grows by 15 percent a year for three years, and then the holding company sells everything for 10x. Your 49 percent of your brand is now worth $2,223,568.

The math above is simple and perhaps a bit rosy. But if you have the ability to sell just a portion of your company and look for a second much higher exit, why not give it a go?

More often than not this is not an option for small online business owners. They've bootstrapped the business and taken very little profit out of it along the way. When they sell, they want and need the proceeds to pay off debt and put some money aside for their next adventure. If that's not you and the option of an equity roll presents itself, it is something worthy of serious consideration.

WORKING CAPITAL PEGS

In most cases I'd say you don't need to worry about a "Peg" (a target) because the vast majority of buyers are not private equity firms. They are entrepreneurs and people leaving the corporate world to become entrepreneurs, and don't seek Pegs like private equity firms do.

But as your business value grows into the $10–20-million-dollar range, you may wind up with a buyer that is quite used to seeking Pegs, along with a variety of the deal structures above—all worked into one deal.

Simply put, the working capital Peg—more often called the "Peg"—is a benchmark, target, or baseline amount of net working capital that is agreed upon by the buyer and the seller and is usually determined toward the end of financial due diligence.

And yes, that means you really don't know how much money

you'll really be left with from your Purchase Price when you go under Letter of Intent.

Your buyer may seek a Peg of one to three months of working capital. Either way, it's a lot of money, and not having it agreed to in advance of the Letter of Intent gives your buyer a strong position to negotiate for more and more in due diligence.

In my eight years of transactions, I have never had a client sign a Letter of Intent that did not specifically outline all of the details of the Purchase Price. In other words, leaving the working capital Peg vague and up to negotiation is foreign to me. But then again, we're typically working on deals that range from $250,000 to $25,000,000. Pegs come into play more often when hitting $10M or more, and rarely exist on the sub $5M deals. It mostly depends on who your buyer is, the deal structure, and what their background is like.

If you sell your e-commerce business to one of the FBA holding or Roll-Up companies and they seek a Peg, odds are they'll seek it in the form of a few months' worth of inventory.

It saddens and frustrates me when entrepreneurs think, "I don't need to pay an Advisor or Broker fee, I'll just reach out to and sell directly to the holding company." In this situation, in their effort to save on the Advisor fee on a $1 million sale, they are giving up a couple of months' worth of inventory in the transaction. And a stability payment, earnout, etc. The few months of inventory given away for free can add up quickly to the Advisor fee, or more. Not to mention the lack of legitimate add-backs they missed out on. And when the seller is selling directly, the holding company has no outside pressure from competitive buyers to pay more for the business or offer a better deal structure.

In summary, if your business is valued in the $100,000 to $10,000,000 range and your buyer is not a private equity firm or holding company, don't worry too much about working capital Pegs. If you do end up with a buyer that seeks one, my advice is to lock in the figure in writing in the Letter of Intent. This way, due diligence is simply a verification of the numbers and risks of the business. It's not designed as a period to renegotiate the terms of the deal.

SELLING YOUR INVENTORY

For good, sellable inventory, the seller should get the landed cost of goods sold on a dollar-for-dollar value. Period. Inventory is paid out at closing *in addition to the purchase price*. There are some exceptions for some private equity firms or holding companies who'll try to get some inventory included in the purchase price, as mentioned above. Everyone else will typically buy it separately.

Now, *landed* cost is a key differentiator here: It's not just the cost of goods sold, because you also have ordered that inventory, paid for that inventory, put it on a plane, truck, train, or boat, and paid the freight fees for it to land at your warehouse of choice. You should be compensated for everything that you spent in that process.

Note: If you don't track freight in costs on an accrual basis in your P&L, you should for this reason! If you just paid $24,000 in freight and it's for the next four months of inventory and you are listing your business for sale next month, cash accounting will reduce your SDE by $24,000 and reduce your overall list price dramatically. If that freight amount is for four months, three are in the future. The SDE for your business is actually $18,000 higher. And the real business value at a 3.5x multiplier is $63,000 higher.

If there's an imbalance of inventory with regard to the purchase price, you may have to negotiate a short-seller note on it as mentioned above. I had a deal last year in which I sold a business for $1.1 million, but it had $600,000 worth of inventory. That's a pretty clear imbalance. The buyer would have to pay a total of $1.7 million for a $1.1 million business, and there was well more than three to four months of inventory.

It generally takes twelve weeks to get inventory from China or Taiwan or wherever you order it from, so having three to four months of inventory from the beginning makes sense. Any more than that, especially if it's not turning quickly, can become a problem.

Inventory aging reports can help you manage your cash flow and inventory so you don't run out, order too much, or order too little.

If your buyer is getting too much inventory or if it's not sellable, it'll tie up their working capital. If you have $600,000 worth of inventory, but three months' worth is only $300,000, they might pay cash for half at closing and then a six-month seller note for the other half. The timing would be based upon how much inventory you have in excess, making it fair and reasonable for both the buyer and seller.

Again, all of these details get specified in the Letter of Intent. LOIs generally do not include amortization schedules, but the general terms of the purchase price and payout structure will all be hashed out and agreed upon before taking another step. Leave out the three-page legal justification of the seller note agreement and just focus on the bullet point version of the terms.

Of course, payment structure is not all there is to negotiate. Every deal is unique, but there are a few key details to sort out before an agreement can be made. That's what we'll work on next.

CHAPTER 16

NEGOTIATING THE DETAILS

The purchase price and terms are just the first parts to work out in the Letter of Intent (LOI). There's still the closing date, asset allocation, the training and transition period, escrow costs, and more.

Once again, no two businesses are alike, and that matters here. This LOI will be different from your next one, which will be different from the one talked about by the person in your mastermind group. But there are a handful of things you'll want to be ready to take into consideration going into every negotiation.

CLOSING DATE

As I've said before, cash deals should close in thirty to forty-five days, and SBA deals should close in sixty to ninety. If you have multiple offers to consider, a cash buyer who can close quickly may win the deal over someone who needs up to ninety days for the SBA loan to come through. But an SBA buyer will still close even if it takes longer, and the silver lining is that you get to hold the business for one to two more months, and earn the extra income before you get your money on closing day.

However, emotions get involved when millions are on the table, just a month or two or three away from hitting your bank account. That leads the vast majority of sellers I've worked with to choose the cash buyer.

It's a less frequent concern, but the time of year that closing happens sometimes comes up as a negotiation point as well. By way of example, I recently had a client who lived part of the year in North Carolina. Halfway through the year, he permanently moved to Florida, where there's no income tax. If he'd closed prior to December 31, he would have owed the state of North Carolina 8 percent on his asset sale. According to him, by closing on January 1, he would owe them nothing. The buyer was fine with waiting until after the first of the year, and it likely saved the seller tens of thousands of dollars in taxes.

ASSET ALLOCATION

Generally speaking, online business transactions in the sub $20M range are asset sales, not stock sales. And the vast majority of the sale is typically considered goodwill, which is the reputation, etc., of the business rather than the physical assets. We generally see an allocation of 80 percent to goodwill and 20 percent to assets. Buyers can negotiate a number of different items here, and paying close attention to these details and consulting with your CPA or tax advisor will put more money in your pocket—after taxes.

How you allocate goodwill versus assets, non-compete or consulting, etc., is really an individual selection and should be based on what you've done with your CPA to date. If you've been depreciating assets purchased that will then be sold in your exit of the business, the value you put toward those assets at closing will impact your taxes due.

Exciting stuff, I know. But it will matter when you exit your business. There is little to no point in writing about this for the next twenty pages because (a) you won't read it and (b) the information will be dated and not applicable to your individual tax situation.

No matter how dull it seems, this component makes a difference in taxes due. Rarely will buyers negotiate and allocate a certain portion of the purchase price to the non-compete (see below). And some buyers will negotiate allocating a certain portion of the purchase price to consulting, because it's a complete write-off. Unfortunately, from the seller's standpoint, it's personal income and taxed at a higher tax bracket.

From time to time, a seller will have a lot of write-offs or losses to offset that income and pay nothing in taxes. You just have to negotiate those consulting agreements in a fair and reasonable way, and make sure it holds up to the letter of the law.

The bottom line here is to use the expertise of your CPA or tax advisor to mitigate your taxes as much as possible.

NON-COMPETE

This one is pretty easy: the buyer does not want to give the seller a whole bunch of money only to have that seller use it to compete against them. A non-compete agreement bars the seller of the business from directly or indirectly competing for the same customers in the same or similar niche.

If you're in the coffee space and I want to buy your business, I won't give you a million dollars just for you to turn around and compete with me. Before I agree to buy, I'll require you to sign a non-compete saying that you will not be in the business of selling coffee online for a certain number of years.

In no way, shape, or form does it block you, as a seller, from selling anything else online, on Amazon, eBay, or any other third-party platform. It doesn't mean you can no longer work in SaaS or create another content site. It just means you can't be in the same space that the business you're selling is in and compete for the same customer.

The reality is that most people who are selling their businesses are ready to move on from that particular niche anyway. They want the next adventure. As such, non-competes aren't a huge sticking point, but they're always something that's negotiated in the Letter of Intent, so that it's clearly defined in the asset purchase agreement.

I try to keep things simple and tie the non-compete to the multiple. If it's a three-time multiple, it seems fair and logical that the non-compete should be for three years. If it's a four-time multiple, the non-compete is four years, etc.

TRAINING AND TRANSITION

After the deal closes and the buyer has full control of your business, it's time to help them understand how to operate your business. As part of the purchase price, you will agree to give a certain number of hours over a certain period of time toward training and transitioning the business. Note that you won't be running the business or working for the buyer. You'll be teaching them, answering their questions, and being there for support.

The best way for you to minimize the amount of work needed

after closing is to have a lot of standard operating procedures (SOPs) in place. These can be written SOPs or recordings of you (or your staff) doing the actual work. As with the video messages earlier in the process, Loom is a great screen recording tool for videos. Agreeing to some time for training and transition support will also instill confidence in the buyer to make a fair and reasonable offer.

Typically, the starting point is "up to forty hours over the first ninety days after closing." It doesn't seem like much, but for the most part I see even that amount not actually fully used.

The "up to" and "over" is simple and clear and doesn't lock anyone into a certain number of hours per day, week, or month. Most of the time is usually in the first few days to weeks after closing, and it trickles off very quickly. Some buyers look for comfort here in this training period and seek more hours or months. They put a lot of money at risk and they want to know that you will be there for them after closing.

Sometimes, they'll ask for up to forty hours over the first ninety days, and then up to five hours per month for another ninety days, just so they know they'll get some sort of response if important questions arise. At the same time, just because it's in the contract doesn't mean a buyer will need or act on it.

Sellers sometimes worry that the buyer will reach out beyond the hours you've established. I advise keeping track of hours for your own purposes. In the event that the hours go above and beyond the initial agreed-upon amount, you can choose to continue to help that person or say you're finished. Some are more than happy to continue helping but expect to be compensated for their time, so they negotiate an hourly amount. Most gear their conversations toward efficiency from the beginning and never run into this problem at all.

In my experience, very few buyers come close to using the allocated time in the purchase agreement. When I sold my business, I negotiated the typical up to forty hours over the first ninety days after closing. My buyer happened to live within two hours of me, and we met during due diligence to go over some things. On the day of closing, I had a physical server in my office that was an asset and part of the sale, so they came over after all the documents were signed to pick it up. We disconnected the server, put it in the car trunk (theirs), and I followed them home to help them set up the network. Effectively, I became their tech person.

All in all, I spent a total of twenty-seven hours working with them in the first ninety days. Once that time expired, they would still reach out now and then. I didn't have to "contractually" respond, but I did every time. We had no reason to be unfriendly, and helping out was the right thing to do. That's how most transition periods work out, provided there is a foundation of trust and fair terms from the beginning.

ESCROW COSTS

In my opinion escrow should be in the middle of most transactions. A rare few attorneys choose to skip it and wire monies to the seller, and then transfer assets. But that is the exception, not the rule. The rule is generally for the buyer to fund escrow, then the seller transfers control of the assets. And then the monies are released from escrow to the seller and training and transition begins.

When it comes to escrow costs, the simplest, plainest, clearest, and fairest thing to do is to simply say that escrow costs, if any, will be split equally between the buyer and the seller. That's all. It's a minor negotiating point, but worth becoming familiar with.

Sometimes, the buyer will negotiate for their attorney to hold escrow, but that person may not have an attorney yet and may not know if it'd be possible. It changes from state to state and attorney to attorney. This can be a negotiation point but it's rarely a sticking point.

There are a couple of online escrow services to use as well, such as zoomescrow.com or escrow.com. The former one was developed by an e-commerce attorney and an entrepreneur quite familiar with online transactions and the need for simple and fair transactions and pricing. The latter has been around for a long time and can get a little pricey on larger transactions.

EXCLUSIVITY

When I offer to buy your business and we agree on the terms, we become exclusive when the LOI is signed and I've provided satisfactory proof of funds. You're no longer allowed to negotiate or share the materials with other buyers or potential buyers. It's just me. I'll put a lot of time, energy, and effort into buying your business, and as a courtesy, you won't continue to shop it around and sell it out from underneath me.

If we've agreed on a purchase price and you are my buyer, and then you try to change the terms in due diligence, even though the numbers are accurate and there is no real reason other than you trying to "beat me up on price," exclusivity is over. I can do anything I want. At least that's what your LOI should say.

The exclusivity period is generally for three to four weeks, and rarely requires an extension, even when due diligence stretches on a little bit longer than planned. By that point, the buyer and seller have established trust. And the seller won't shop it around that close to the end—we all want to make it to the closing table by that point. Extension language can be added to the LOI though. It gets a little complex and varies from deal to deal.

With an SBA deal, you would have that initial period that allows you to get through underwriting and receive a commitment letter. Depending upon the lender, it might be thirty or forty-five days. After the commitment letter, exclusivity would automatically extend through closing.

Overall, the exclusivity period is more of a "feel good" component for the buyer. They will want to know you're not shopping around for a better buyer or deal.

CHAPTER 17

NAVIGATING DUE DILIGENCE

No seller really looks forward to due diligence. It's invasive, tedious, and a little frightening. You're sharing years of bank statements, vendor invoices, merchant statements, and almost every possible document that led to the profit and loss statements, sometimes amounting to thirty-six individual PDFs—three years' worth—for each of those types of documents filed into three different folders. You might be revealing code, doing screen shares, and sharing a whole host of other "under the hood" components of your business.

On top of the financial statements, you also have to dive into inventory, aging reports, descriptions of your growth opportunities, and any SKUs, apps, or content that you've prepared for launch in the next twelve months, and much more.

I liken it to the most vulnerable and invasive routine doctor's procedures that most of us experience on an annual basis. You can fill in the blanks here. We all know it's coming, and that it leads to important "peace of mind" types of things, but that doesn't mean we have to like it. Preparation helps.

For due diligence, preparation is ongoing.

Sometimes business owners think this is just a data dump—all kinds of documents just thrown into one folder and left for the buyer to figure out what's what. But that's not the way EXIT-preneurs should go about it. Everything we do, including but not limited to due diligence, is intended to help the buyer go through the process with ease.

When an EXITpreneur reaches due diligence, they're prepared to hand all of their documentation over via a secure folder online, with files organized by category, ready at the request of the buyer. They have gathered and filed all required documents and anything that will verify what they've presented in the financials and client interview. Trademarks and patents are made ready, labeled so they're sequential and easy to view, just like we talked about in Chapter 8.

As a refresher, labeling your documents properly is the first important step. The bank will likely send December's statement file labeled *December 2020* rather than the more efficient *12.2020*, which means you have some reorganizing to do. Here's what a folder with the bank statements will look like if you don't rename them with numbers:

April-2020
August-2020
December-2020
February-2020
January-2020
July-2020
June-2020
March-2020

May-2020
November-2020
October-2020
September-2020

It may seem like a minor thing, but to a buyer, clear and efficiently labeled due diligence files can make everything easier—and that's good for you too.

If you take an extra few minutes with your files and rename them with numbers, they'll fall in sequential order and make due diligence just a little easier for your buyer. And sometimes "just a little" makes an enormous difference.

Here's how to rename the same files as above:

1. 2020 Bank Statement
2. 2020 Bank Statement
3. 2020 Bank Statement
4. 2020 Bank Statement
5. 2020 Bank Statement
6. 2020 Bank Statement
7. 2020 Bank Statement
8. 2020 Bank Statement
9. 2020 Bank Statement
10. 2020 Bank Statement
11. 2020 Bank Statement
12. 2020 Bank Statement

With numbers instead of letters, the months fall sequentially, and that is easier to follow when looking at hundreds of files. But then, we don't dump all of the files into one folder. No— that's a data dump, and that's bad.

Once you have your files properly named, you'll need to add them to properly named folders as well. Sticking with the bank statement example, here's how I would name the bank statement folders:

2020-Bank Statements
2019-Bank Statements
2018-Bank Statements

Again, with the numbers in front they'll fall sequentially.

Every buyer is different, just like every business. Therefore, you won't know the full list of due diligence files your buyer will be requesting until they request it. Some look for simple verifications, while others dig really deep and require a near rebuilding of the P&L, live screen shares, etc.

To prepare for your eventual due diligence, I'd suggest you compile the following statements renamed and organized as suggested above. And save them to your preferred cloud tool (e.g., Google Drive) so there is no risk of losing them when your morning cup of coffee destroys your hard drive.

Shoot for three years of the following, if possible.

- Bank Statements
- Credit Card Processing Statements
- Vendor Invoices
- Third-Party Seller Statements (e.g., Amazon, eBay)
- Tax Returns
- Copies of Incorporation Docs
- Copies of all Contracts
- Payroll Reports, or equivalent for VAs and contractors

Your P&Ls with monthly views would have been provided already in the original Business Summary or Deck, but you could add them to the above as well. The more prepared you are for the hectic pace of due diligence, the easier the process will be.

And remember, you still have to be operating your business during this entire time. You don't want to take your eye off the ball there. Declining revenues will have more of an impact on your buyer's decision than anything else. So get organized now for your eventual due diligence so you don't drop any balls along the way.

THE PROCESS OF DUE DILIGENCE

Just as no two businesses are alike, buyers are unique as well. Your specific combination of variables will shape a due diligence process that meets your buyer's needs. In the most detail-oriented cases, they will take every shred of information that you provide and recreate a profit and loss statement from scratch. Most will focus on the last twelve months, verified through third-party documents and view-only permission of your Google analytics and third-party seller accounts. They will schedule live phone calls for you to log on and pull up certain reports to screen share them instead of printed reports that can be forged.

Your buyer may hire a due diligence firm to run the process for them, or they will use their team to conduct it themselves. Others know that SBA underwriters do a great deal of verification and due diligence through tax returns, which becomes a secure verification point on its own. If the buyer does some due diligence, the bank does its own, and then a third-party valuation firm is hired as well, that's triple verification for the buyer to be completely comfortable with the deal.

To clarify, the value of a business is based on the trailing twelve months, but the buyer could seek three years of due diligence documents. If I show you that a business has grown 25 percent year over year, you'll pay the most attention to the last twelve months because that's where the value is partly derived from. That's where the math goes back to—a multiple times discretionary earnings.

The multiple that's applied is based upon the trends over the last three years, so if it's up by 25 percent over the last three years, for example, that multiple could be pushed a little higher. If you're at a two-time multiple, it's probably because the trends are going down and the risk is higher. If you grossed $3 million in 2016, $2.5 million in 2017, and only $2 million in 2018, your buyer will want to see financials for all three of those years, with a monthly view so seasonal comparisons can be made. Some people don't want to do it for all three years; they're good with two, or they may just spot check year two and year three and look at deposits randomly throughout the year. They'll still ask for the material. They'll absolutely ask for year one, they're very likely to ask for year two, and there's a good chance they'll ask for year three. Every buyer is different.

DEALING WITH ERRORS

Last January, I listed a business for a seller who was confident that his books were in perfect order. He'd been diligent about his financials, and it all looked good in our valuation process. He went under contract in February and expected due diligence to be a smooth process.

Unfortunately, there were some simple but significant problems, just oversights made by a bookkeeper on currency conversions. But they added up. Over the course of the trailing twelve months, revenues that were gathered overseas should have been converted to USD in his accounting software, but they were not.

It was a frustrating, emotional discovery. The owner was floored. He felt like it misrepresented the way he conducts business. He felt like his character was at risk.

The thing is with that deal, very little was actually at risk at that point.

That deal was under LOI at a three-and-a-half-time multiple, which turned the error into about a $17,000 difference on the purchase price. But because the buyer and seller were looking out for each other, emotions were easily overpowered by math and logic. The buyer suggested a drop on purchase price by the $17,000 amount. Meanwhile, during the three or four weeks that it'd been under LOI, the business SDE value had grown by about $23,000, and they agreed to no change in the purchase price regardless of the bookkeeper's error. They liked and respected each other. That respect resulted in a great relationship after closing that far outweighed the small short-term benefit the buyer would have had if he'd pushed hard to get a price reduction.

Even the best business owners could wind up in due diligence with some wrong data. It's not intentional. There's just a lot of data flying around that requires a lot of verification. Don't take it personally if your buyer finds errors in due diligence—just work together to solve the problem and get the deal back on track.

I'm often asked how much we have to prepare for renegotiation, and the answer is in your initial numbers. Your financials should be correct from the onset. You should have answered all the appropriate questions in the written client interview. The buyer should know everything they need to know about the business. There *should* be no surprises.

When you prepare your business in that way—to be as close to right as possible from the very beginning—any honest mistakes that pop up shouldn't kill the deal. And then renegotiation is a simple adjustment based on the new math and logic, not anything personal at all.

WHAT ABOUT DUE DILIGENCE FIRMS?

The responsibility of verification of all the numbers is truly up to the buyer, after a Letter of Intent (LOI) is executed. Although I have walked you through the process here, I am not part of a due diligence firm, nor is any Advisor I know of. We can spot check top-line and bottom-line numbers, but we do not go through the entire process for a buyer.

Our job is to prepare the seller of the business for what's to come—the financial probe that will happen once under LOI. We make sure they understand that everything they give us will be verified once under LOI, then advise them as they work hard to get it right. You can't fake good numbers. Sometimes I'll catch obvious things in my spot-check, but a deep dive is up to the buyer. If you're worried about complete fabrication, you haven't been through due diligence before. No seller in their right mind will lie about everything, knowing what's to come.

Intentional lying and unintentional oversights are quite different, however, so I always recommend that the buyer hire a due diligence firm to help them pore over the financials. Especially if they are unfamiliar with the space. The seller, on the other hand, typically has enough going on while listing the business. Run it professionally, prepare to the best of your ability, and work with the due diligence firm that the buyer hires, rather than trying to hire your own first.

RUNNING A BUSINESS DURING DUE DILIGENCE

Once due diligence begins, it can take roughly one to eight weeks to complete, depending on the size of the deal. The worst of it for the seller will be catching up on any disorganized documentation. When I sold my last business, I distinctly remember complaining to my wife that I was working harder selling my business than I was running it. I was working more hours on tedious things that I had never paid much attention to. Let my mistakes save you some time.

Sometimes this is a big ask for an underprepared seller. They have lives and families, and now I'm asking them to give me information about their financials to firm up the seller's discretionary earnings, then throwing more record-keeping and filing on top of it.

The better you can prepare for what's coming, the better return you'll get on your investments of time and risk in building your businesses. Then, when due diligence does eventually come around, you'll be ready. Buyers have the right to ask deep, probing questions, because they're ready to put their life savings on the line for it. They need to make sure their investments are safe.

Even if people ask you cold questions, answer them. Dig up any missing paperwork. Go through whatever wringer the firm has for you, and then have a drink or whatever you do to relax at the end of the day. It's only a few weeks of your life—you'll survive it, and at the end of it all, there will be money in your bank account like you've never seen before.

CHAPTER 18

ATTORNEYS AND ADVISORS

My twenty-eight-year-old client had a $750,000 deal on the table. It was a much higher multiple than the business deserved, and he had excellent, cash-only terms. But it fell through.

His problems started when he showed up to the table for the asset purchase agreement with multiple attorneys. Even worse, they were his parents, his fiancé in law school, and an Advisor from his graduate school. They went after a few stomachache clauses like rabid dogs. After weeks of frustration, the buyer walked away, unwilling to take on all the risk without the seller holding any at all.

Once you're part way through due diligence and feeling confident that the deal will close, it's time to hire an attorney to firm up the asset purchase agreement. Any sooner, and you'll waste money hiring an attorney for the non-binding Letter of Intent. Wait until you're confident the deal will move forward, then lock in an agreement to hire a competent contract attorney who's familiar with the online space.

Early on, for our smaller deals in the sub-$250,000 range, I thought it was acceptable for the buyer or seller to just tweak a template asset purchase agreement to their liking. Today, I rarely make that exception, especially now that values have gone up so much. If you're spending $1 million and are hesitant to spend $5,000–$10,000 on an attorney, something's up. Just accept this expense as part of the process. Peace of mind is worth so much more than that set of fees.

You'll spend time going back and forth with attorneys to get the language right on the asset purchase agreement, which usually starts with a buyer's template modified by their attorney. I've watched as a single buyer purchased millions worth of businesses using the same attorney. That attorney fights for her client on certain points every time. That same attorney often represents our sellers, and takes the opposite stance on those same points, arguing against them when she represents the seller. It's quite humorous! The key is to hire a good contract attorney familiar with the online space.

Do not hire your mother, father, brother, sister, aunt, uncle, cousin, best friend, or best friend's wife.

Do not assume that you are fine without an attorney.

Do not decide that you've "got this" and can list and sell alone.[6]

Trust your attorney and the process—it's worth the time it takes to get each little piece of the agreement right.

6　Arguably, you have enough information here to make your way through a deal without a Broker if you had to. However, thinking back to the business that I sold, I don't recommend it. The extra support is invaluable.

STOMACHACHE CLAUSES

You as the seller are liable for everything that happens in the business up to the minute that you close the transaction and you have no more customers purchasing your services or products. The buyer is responsible for all their new customers and services from minute one after you close. There's a clear divide between the past and the future.

Regardless of the divide, a customer of the brand could sue the new owner, regardless that they bought the product or service six to twelve months ago. To hold you, the seller, liable for that possibility up to a certain dollar amount, stomachache clauses are added—making you liable up to a certain dollar amount if the issue occurs. This is where attorneys get into fights, lobbing emails at each other until you get them on a phone call. Nine times out of ten, a phone call will resolve most issues. That tenth time is usually when an attorney is a friend or family member and can't see the deal logically.

The asset purchase agreement should be drafted to protect both the buyer and seller. For the buyer, a significant investment of this kind deserves a legally binding agreement to protect against fraud and damages. For the seller, knowing their millions of dollars won't be taken away at any point lets them sleep at night. Attorneys help us secure the win/win we crafted.

FROM DUE DILIGENCE TO CLOSING

If due diligence turns up information that reveals the discretionary earnings are much lower than the LOI accounted for, the buyer would not be required to move forward with the asset purchase agreement. The buyer can walk away or renegotiate a price in due diligence. If the requirements in the asset purchase agreement are not to the satisfaction of the buyer or seller, their attorney will advise them and they will have the ability to walk away. In this sense, LOIs are non-binding, and fully contingent upon due diligence and a detailed asset purchase agreement.

However, pieces of the LOI, such as exclusivity, *are* binding. You can't shop the business around, though I can't imagine you wanting to. Once a business is under contract, the seller is excited to get to closing.

Generally, closing comes shortly after signing the asset purchase agreement. You'll watch for the approaching target closing date in the LOI, and if due diligence is on track, engage with the attorney as you near the halfway period. Attorneys have lives, holidays happen, and vacations take place. So there is no hard and fast rule that you must close (or even get to close) on the date outlined in the LOI. In fact, almost every LOI I have worked on refers to the closing date as "XYZ date, or otherwise agreed upon closing date by both parties."

Once the asset purchase agreement is fully agreed upon and signed, closing will happen and the purchase price funds will be wired to the escrow account. If you have an all-cash million-dollar purchase price plus $200,000 of inventory, that $1.2 million gets wired into the escrow account, and the escrow attorney will confirm receipt. Then you'll begin the transition of the assets from the seller to the buyer as planned.

It's rare that the attorneys will recommend skipping escrow and wiring funds directly to the seller then transferring the assets of the business. It does happen, though, and it can be a bit nerve-racking for the buyer. In my experience attorneys who work this way are used to buyers and sellers sitting at a closing table together. This rarely happens when selling an online business, so having an escrow attorney or service in the middle increases the comfort level of all parties involved.

Back in 2010, I hired a fair attorney for about $4,000. Today, it ranges from $5,000 to a rather high and unusual $15,000 for a simple asset purchase agreement. The best way to know you have a good attorney is not by their price range, but through references and referrals.

LAST WORD ON ADVISORS

In January 2016, I went to an E-commerce Fuel event in Savannah, Georgia, and one of the presenters was from a foreign country, swore a lot, and was all-around entertaining. As he and I mulled around over a drink after his presentation, he started to share some of his insights.

He said, "Joe, you know what? I lay it all out there. I give all of the information on how to do search engine optimization on my website, YouTube, and forums for free. And at the end of the day, people realize how much work it is. Even though I've told them exactly how to do it and what to do, they hire me instead, so they can keep doing what they're doing, running their businesses."

That's what the best Advisors do. Yet I watch people run their businesses, making sure they don't drop any balls. Then when their reward is just around the corner, I see them selling their businesses and negotiating through due diligence with no guidance at all—just some bragging that their friend did and a blog post about multiples.

In the vernacular of my friend in Georgia, I think these business owners are f#$k#%g nuts.

Just because three of your friends wound up with seller notes or an earnout doesn't mean that you will. What you heard at a mastermind event or group or forum isn't everything you need to know to sell your business. The objective in this book is to give you the tools to make better decisions with what is likely your most valuable asset. It's not to replace the direct support and guidance of highly qualified attorneys and Advisors.

Even for EXITpreneurs who have done this over and over again, you'll still learn new lessons every time. You'll treat each new deal as though it's something fresh and different. You'll become a better entrepreneur with more experience. *And you'll be more prepared for an Advisor or Broker to help you successfully get across the finish line.*

Maybe—*maybe*—you'll reach a point where you can do this on your own. But the truth of the matter is that serious buyers often tell me they prefer to buy businesses from Advisors and Brokers. Why? Because they do all of the hard work for them. They ask all the right questions, get all the answers, and get the profit and loss statements pulled together in the right format with all the data so the buyer can make better decisions more quickly.

When they buy directly from sellers, they have to do ten times as much work and look for discounts because of it. Similarly, when you sell a business on your own, you don't do a deep dive into your own business, have thorough presentations, or have the ability to compare your business to hundreds that have actually sold, and with what terms. This gets ugly fast.

With the business properly valued and packaged up for sale, Advisors are also going to help you sort through the buyers that come to the table, educate them on how the process works, and make sure they really can and will buy your business, with the right terms, if it's a good fit.

Portfolio buyers sometimes know what questions to ask, but non-portfolio buyers purchasing businesses for the first time don't know much of anything. The questions never end, and the offers rarely come, at least in any form that is appealing to the seller. Some don't get through due diligence, which is a colossal waste of everyone's time—the sellers, buyers, and anyone who skipped over the ugly details of the business.

New buyers can work with new sellers, and any other configuration therein, as long as they fit within the true buyer hierarchy: the capable buyer who understands deal structures and a balanced amount of risk, and the non-capable buyer with little cash or realistic expectations on what really works for a seller.

That's really it. Any kind of structure or experience level can turn into a great deal with the right expectations and preparation.

While buyers operate on math and logic, sellers often struggle to separate emotion from their decisions. Case in point: sellers sometimes prefer buyers with experience because it seems like it will be easier for them after closing, or cash buyers so they will get there faster. This isn't necessarily wrong, but it usually comes at the cost of a lower value.

Last year, I helped an owner list his business that was perfect in a dozen ways. I wanted to list it at a 3.5 multiple, but he asked for a 3.3. We did it, and he got ten offers, including one that was $150,000 higher than all others. Ultimately, he accepted a 3.5 offer from a cash buyer who had experience running his type of business so it would be easier for him in due diligence and training afterward.

The highest offer by $150,000 was an SBA deal and would have taken longer to close. Logically the seller should have accepted that offer and captured another month's worth of profit during the longer due diligence and closing process. He was all emotion though. He had some personal things going on that impacted his focus on business, and he was tired and worn out—and just wanted to get to closing.

A good Advisor will manage your expectations and help you keep your emotions in check so that you know exactly what you're getting into, but the final say is always going to be yours. At the end of the day, if you feel great about your deal and are prepared for whatever comes next, then we've all done our job.

LISTING ON YOUR OWN

You may be thinking, I can do this without an Advisor and skip the fee! One of the problems with this thinking is that going direct to one buyer takes all of the competitive pressure off them when it comes to negotiating the deal. They know you've reached out to them and that the general marketplace is not also considering your business as a purchase. They know you are not getting ten offers, but just one. And that one offer will not be as clean or as sweet a deal for you because they are not competing against others.

There is a lot to be said for getting a lot of potential buyers to look at your business when it comes to getting close to or at asking price—and with terms that are much more attractive than you'd get when listing direct or presenting to just one buyer.

In my experience properly calculating SDE and the list price, and presenting a business to the general marketplace of educated buyers, brings so much more value in terms of purchase price, deal structure, process, and peace of mind...and they all outweigh a fee that you'll pay to an Advisor at closing. In other words, you'll earn more, even after the fee.

Now, take that all with a grain of salt, because I'm in the M&A world and am one of the people that earns those fees. But hopefully you've gotten to know, like, and trust me now that you've read this far. You still just know enough to be dangerous, and my hope is to keep you away from some of those dangers.

CHAPTER 19

WHAT HAPPENS NEXT?

You found a great buyer and went under LOI. You made it through due diligence. You signed the asset purchase agreement and were notified that the money was in escrow. You closed, handed over control of the assets, and "went home" with no business and no money.[7]

It isn't until the money is finally released from escrow that the weight finally lifts off your shoulders.

When I say *finally*, I mean it takes about one to three business days (though it can take longer, depending on the deal and buyer). But it might as well be a year. All the technical details are done. Everything that's hard is over. You've been through a string of emotions already, but then you hold your breath walking away from closing and check your bank account over and over to make sure it's all done. There's nothing like that sigh of relief when you hit refresh and a whole bunch of money hits your bank account.

---

7   When I sold my business, it took a whole weekend to see any money. I try to never close on Fridays anymore because of that.

And, for the record, "a whole bunch" is relative too. Every business sale, from $28,000 to $28 million, is worth celebrating. There are feelings of relief and joy and excitement every single time.

To review, here's the general sequence of events before money hits your bank account:

1. You go under LOI.
2. Due diligence (occurs over two to four weeks).
3. You negotiate and sign the APA (two weeks).
4. The buyer wires funds to escrow (within a day or so of signing the APA).
5. The escrow firm or attorney confirms the money has been received and notifies the buyer and seller.
6. The seller and buyer work together to transfer the assets of the business to the buyer.
7. Both the buyer and seller notify escrow that the assets have transferred and to release funds.
8. The escrow firm wires the funds to the seller.
9. Transition and training begin.

But then what?

When a seller closes on their first deal—or their biggest deal yet, or really anytime the money hits their bank—I suggest a little celebration ritual for them. Go to the ATM, withdraw some money, and get a receipt with the balance on it. Print that out and frame it or carry it in your wallet forever. Alternatively, log into your online bank account and take a screenshot, then frame it. Either works! You've done something that few people will ever do, and it deserves commemoration.

The next step is to follow the plan you had already laid out for what comes next in your life. In this final chapter, we'll look at ways to shape that plan and then stick to it.

PLAN YOUR NEXT STEPS

The short answer for next steps is that you have to do the math and know what your options are. Every situation is different, but one thing is true for us all: if you start scrambling, you won't be as thoughtful in your next adventure. (Ask me how I know.)

Glad you asked. When I sold my business just after the Great Recession, I let time pass without much of a plan. It wasn't until I filed my tax returns that I thought, "Oh yeah, I should probably have some sort of line of credit—*right* now." With almost seven figures in equity on my house, I applied for a home equity line of credit…and was denied. Why?

You don't have a job, Mr. Valley.

Oh, that's right. Fantastic.

Instead of regrouping and taking my time, I quickly bought a business that I shouldn't have. It looked easy. It checked the cash flow boxes I thought I had figured out. But I didn't have a plan. It was bad timing and a bad choice of business with a bad algorithm update that sank rankings and lost me a quarter of a million dollars—all in just six months.

If you're an EXITpreneur who is primed for your next business venture, you'll need to give yourself room to choose the next startup and get it off the ground.

What you get from the sale helps determine your options afterward and how soon you need to get a plan in place. Someone might sell and never have to work again for the rest of their life, while someone else might sell and be back at work in just a few months. Factor this into your planning as soon as you start setting goals for the sale.

If your financial runway after the sale is short, start planning the next project before your first exit is complete. If you have a longer financial runway with very low overhead, you can take a longer amount of time off.

TAKE TIME TO CELEBRATE

No matter how much time you have, make sure some of it is spent relaxing and celebrating. But be careful not to overdo the celebration of your sale for too long, or it could send you back into the workforce with empty pockets.

One of my clients—Joe, who is in the process of selling as I write this—has rock-bottom low overhead. After his sale, he's taking a full month off to go fishing in his soon-to-be-purchased boat. He knows he'll work again, but he also knows that he can put his phone down and relax entirely without worrying about money.

Another client of mine who sold their business—a couple, Brian and Janine—already have a new business making forty sales a day (and climbing rapidly), which is so small compared to what they did before that it feels like taking time off. Your time off might be to work less, rest for weeks on end, or just take a good weekend to relax before getting onto the next adventure.

No matter what it looks like, you need that time to take a beat and think about what you've accomplished. Not only did you make that $200,000, $2 million, or $20 million sale, but you now have the skillset to do it again. The only thing standing between you and your *next* exit is burnout. And burnout is a very real obstacle.

People who sell their businesses after running them too long, when they are trending down, generally don't earn the values they need to match their lifestyles. They have to take almost more risk starting or buying their next business because they're doing it as the cash runs out.

You've been going full steam ahead for years on a business, putting money into it to make it grow to the point that you can sell. During all that time, you don't get mental breaks. It's not part of the gig for most entrepreneurs. The freedom and flexibility we have as business owners makes it look easy from the outside, but the reality is that we never fully turn our minds off the venture. Even while traveling and enjoying our own schedule, we're checking sales and responding to emails and putting out fires every day. We sleep less and, in a lot of ways, work more. The work never ends.

Pausing to celebrate gives you the mental rest you need to be able to start over. When you take time off after the sale, it allows you to reflect on what you've been through in the last few years. You can think about what you liked and didn't like and how that might shape your next adventure.

We don't get to love everything we do, but we can plan to minimize our exposure to the tasks and roles we don't like once we've been through it and can take some time to identify those things and shape our next steps around them.

Take time to pat yourself on the back. Buy yourself a treat—

whether it's ice cream or a boat—and take a breather before life gets busy again. Just be sure to run the math first so you don't spend all your money.

HOW MUCH MONEY WILL I SEE?

I've said this a thousand times over the years. "It's not how much you sell your business for that matters most, it's how much you keep." And inevitably this leads to some quick math and recommendations to dive deeper.

To be clear, if I were to attempt to tell you exactly what you'll be left with after your Advisor fee and taxes...I would be wrong. Why? I don't think everyone reading this lives in Texas, for instance. Or California, where the capital taxes are dramatically different than the Lone Star State. In addition, your personal tax situation may be dramatically different than the millionth reader of this book. (Yep, I'm being optimistic!)

Who you choose to work with as an Advisor will impact what you ultimately sell the business for, the type of deal structure and buyer, and the efficiency of the process. What you have left over after fees and taxes will vary wildly. The fees are often a variation of the Lehman Scale. Most often, the Modern Lehman Scale. Taxes, though—that's a completely different story.

Everyone's situation is different, and both federal and state taxes have to be taken into consideration. The best thing you can do is plan, read, and plan. And get lots of advice from CPAs and tax mitigation experts.

To simplify things, you should be looking at capital gains taxes, not personal income taxes. If that doesn't help just a little bit, you need to educate yourself further on the difference.

At the time of this writing, the federal capital gain taxes are at the 20 percent rate for higher income earners (>$441,451). These rates go down dramatically depending on your income. You've also got to add 3.8 percent for the net investment tax due to Obamacare. Compare these figures to personal income taxes at a comparable 35 percent if married and filing jointly—and you'll see a difference of 11.2 percent.

On a $1 million transaction, that's a tax difference of $112,000. And we haven't even attempted adding in state taxes.

I know some extreme measures taken to reduce state taxes. One entrepreneur, who planned his exit years in advance, moved from California, where he would have paid roughly 13 percent in state capital gains taxes on the sale of his business, to Texas, where the capital gains rate was zero at the time of his sale.

You have worked incredibly hard to grow your business. You've risked everything and now it's time to sell. You may not like studying taxes—very few people do. But if you put just 1/100th of the effort into understanding your personal taxes situation on an exit that you have into running your business, you'll find the payoff to be extraordinary.

GET READY TO REPEAT

The woman who cried when her $28,000 business sold had only worked three or four hours a day on it. It didn't make a lot of money, but she was able to take that windfall and focus on her kids for a while. With her goals met, not to mention the knowledge that she was helping someone else, that sale was life-changing for her.

In another sale, an EXITpreneur sold her online business for $2.6 million. She immediately started building another business. But first, she stroked a check to pay off $200,000 in student loan debt that would have plagued her for a decade or more. She can make less each month without hurting her lifestyle, because she no longer has that fixed debt amount dogging her.

As I write this today, an EXITpreneur in his thirties is financially set for life and has already taken yet another business as far as he wants to. The next level of growth would require hiring people with a different mentality, resources, staffing, and worldwide operations. The sale of this business will de-risk his personal life by eliminating another round of overhead, buildings, inventory, liabilities, and time, then secure finances for the next generation or two of his family.

EXITpreneurs want to do this again and again because it's in our blood. Each time we do it, we get better and smarter. We reflect on what we liked and didn't, what worked and what failed, what was hard and what came naturally, what we were good at and what we struggled with. With each new adventure, we can tweak and fine-tune our process a bit more. Then, when we get to the top, or close to it, we can hand it off to someone else and start over with even more lessons learned.

What is "the top"? Only you can answer that.

Looking back, I could have taken that first product I launched in January of 1998 one hundred percent online if I'd stuck with it, but it would have grown beyond my level of competence at the time. I would have been miserable.

Victor kept discovering new levels of his own potential. He sold one business for $7,500, another for $20,000, a third for over $200,000, and another for nearly $9 million. His next goal is a billion-dollar exit. He's learned so much and is so driven, I have no doubt he'll come close to, if not exceed, his goal.

This begs the next question: if selling at the top is so great, what happens when I bottom out?

Maybe you've heard someone talk about losing $7 million and going bankrupt, or other giant fails. Maybe you're still spinning out over the story of my $250,000 loss—and I didn't even mention how I lost just as much in real estate at the same time. I understand the fear. Do I see massive losses and failures among EXITpreneurs? Yes. But you learn from these moments and grow. You don't give up. You fight and move on. You share that experience with others.

You're on this path because it's part of who you are, and you can't succeed or grow without failure. Thinking in terms of an EXITpreneur won't help you avoid failure, but it will help you start out with more lessons learned, plans in place, and a clearer vision of the future.

BOOTSTRAP, GROW, SELL, REPEAT

Once you know the process, you can repeat it. You'll find the next SaaS business to build, content site, or product to build a brand around, before your financial runway gives out. You'll have some money set aside from the first sale to inject into the next one, so your bootstraps won't feel so tight. Then you'll follow the same path to growth and an eventual exit as you did before, but this time with better organization and financials from the beginning.

You might stay close to your niche because it's something you care about. Joe wants to stick with fishing when he gets back from his trip. Meanwhile, Brian and Janine are category agnostic. They just want something that's as defensible as possible so they can sell it at a higher value and higher multiple than the last one.

What EXITpreneurs learn and experience from selling their businesses makes them better entrepreneurs when it's time to start up again. They can build something with the next buyer in mind, without ever hitting that feeling of being stuck indefinitely. They have goals. They see milestones. The process of preparing the business to sell isn't as painful, because it's familiar.

They start with a good bookkeeper, they track good metrics, and they separate brands and accounts from the beginning. They expect it to take twenty-four months before they can sell at a fair value, and they know what kind of windfall is waiting for them at the end.

With your first business, you're the brand-new mom who has to boil the pacifier every time it falls on the floor. Two or three businesses down the road, you become the mom who spits on the fallen pacifier to clean it off and pops it back in the crying baby's mouth.

The stress just isn't the same after you've been there, done that, and survived.

BETTER FOR EVERYONE

From my perspective as an Advisor, there's a significant difference between someone who "decides" to sell and an "EXITpreneur."

First-time sellers have everything riding on that business, with their emotions all over the place. When the financials are inevitably in rough shape, it diminishes the value of the business that they thought they had. They're sometimes focused on the wrong things, like choosing an Advisor who promises to drop his or her commission instead of one who understands a proper add-back schedule and can earn you more even with the full fee. Experience brings knowledge, which creates peace of mind and a smoother process.

When I think of the most prepared EXITpreneurs, Paul comes to mind.

Even though he was a CPA prior to his entrepreneurial life, he outsourced to a highly qualified e-commerce bookkeeper from the beginning. He did a great job with branding. He was likable. Then he sold after about thirty months, when the business was trending up and there were still a ton of growth opportunities.

By choosing the pain of the EXITpreneur's playbook, Paul wound up without much pain at all. The process was smoother, and time flew by as he kept moving toward his goals.

Knowing what you're building toward shapes the decisions you make every day. Do we spin out about bad customer service emails? No, we find a way to appease them without tarnishing our reputation and risking the sale. Do we need to shoot another video? Yes, because content is education and education is what we're eventually selling. It pulls every last ounce of ego out of the business. This isn't about you anymore. It's about what you're building for your buyer—and that is the best, arguably only, way to make your dreams a reality.

CONCLUSION

THE INCREDIBLE EXITPRENEUR

YOUR STORY

It's time to insert your story here, right where you are at this moment in time.

You don't have to find a bunch of capital. You don't have to win the lottery. You don't have to grow your business beyond your level of competence and then hope someone rescues you. You don't have to be on this treadmill forever.

You just have to do the work.

The plain, boring, unsexy work of documentation and planning and adjusting and refining. Training.

The everyday minor-details work—that will turn into a bigger win than you can imagine.

This is the secret to being an EXITpreneur: you're building a great business, not so you can sell it for a million dollars, but so someone else can buy it for a million and then grow it to three.

Being an EXITpreneur is about being thoughtful as you build your business, not just grinding out the next month's earnings. It's not about getting someone else's money, but about putting a great opportunity in front of them that will allow you to move onto your next one.

Choose the pain of creating something worth buying.

Learn what details are important to get right. Read this book again. Watch webinars and videos, and talk with Advisors. Like any good training regimen, once you get over the initial pain and start to see the benefits and results, it becomes addictive. When you see the result of a great sale within an easier process to a better buyer, you're going to come back for more. It becomes a mission—a way to do some good in the world.

There are no shortcuts. If you try to find them, they'll come back to burn you. You won't achieve your goals this time, except for your ability to learn and do better the next time.

The secret to being an EXITpreneur is the secret to all success in life: when you think of others first and do what's in their best interest, it comes around to benefit you in a big way too.

WILL YOU OR WON'T YOU?

Remember how I ran into all of those chargebacks right after I said, "I got this"? (See Chapter 2.) I wasn't the first or last business owner to run into that problem. Not only is it a financial mess, but it's entirely unpleasant. The customer says, "I've been fraudulently charged for this item," so the credit card company refunds them, charges you, and marks it against your business. You can look up the individual, fill out a form, send a letter, and win the chargeback. But it's intentionally difficult and not always worth the effort.

A couple of summers ago, an EXITpreneur client of mine was on his second e-commerce business in a very specific niche. It had grown like crazy, including a recurring revenue aspect that happened every twelve months. Without a reminder about the recurring fee, customers were complaining and chargebacks were high.

He called me with a plan. He decided to use one merchant provider for the first $100,000 in sales. If chargebacks got close to the limit, he'd start using the second, and third and so on.

Reader: This was not a good plan. It was a house of cards.

His business would still be sellable like this, but the risk level was going to hurt him significantly. Buyers would see that they had to create a system to work around the merchant provider terms and services, and the fear of blacklisting would pull down the value.

My response was simple, painful, and born of experience: "Why don't you just fix the underlying problem and remind the customer of the upcoming charge?"

"Because sales will go down."

"But so will your chargebacks. Yes, you will lose some legitimate sales when you remind your customers of the upcoming withdrawal, but if the chargeback problem continues, you're going to lose everything. Why not take a little extra time to build a solid business with the new business owner in mind?"

As an Advisor, I wasn't ready to take on a business with shaky foundations. Instead, I advised him to move his exit goalpost out by another twelve to eighteen months. His discretionary earnings could go down, but his multiple would be higher because it would be a legitimate business that wasn't full of risk. Ultimately, he'd be taking care of the most important people, the customers, and preparing the business for the new owners to run without massive headaches. Fix the model, take care of the customer who will then take care of you, and build a better business for the next owner. Everyone wins.

Since that call, this EXITpreneur has done the right thing and thought of the next owner of the business. He and his partners went above and beyond fixing any chargeback issues and taking care of the customer first. They hired developers to create a back end that would make the business easier to manage and better for buyers to take over. And as of this writing, the business is under LOI and deep in due diligence with a clear line of sight toward closing. The value of the business for the buyers is incredible, with a dramatic upside. For the sellers, it's another successful exit—a truly incredible exit.

When you're immersed in a stressful situation, it's hard to see anything but your next paycheck. A quick exit, on shifty terms, can feel like a way out, but it may not be the best way out. Even if you manage to find a buyer under less-than-ideal circumstances, will it set you up for your next venture? Will it be a transaction you feel good about? Will it become something you're proud of and happy to repeat?

You're the only one who can answer that. You're the only one who can choose that pain, for your own good and the good of everyone your business reaches.

STEP INTO ACTION

You can only learn so much from books. They are brilliant resources to refer back to, but there will always be little nuances that are only properly conveyed through spoken conversation.

Good Advisors are there to help, first and foremost. They'll give you the kind of education you received here, but specific to your business. It's all of the details we sorted out in the book conveyed by someone who's been through the process as an Advisor many times. It's someone telling you what current market rates are for businesses like yours. It's running the financial Key Metrics to see what things look like compared to other businesses in the same niche.

They want to talk to you. They want to understand your business. They want to answer all of your questions, and to support you all along your journey. If you choose the right Advisor, they'll be there when you're really ready to sell your business too.

Your revenue isn't too low to talk to someone. Your business isn't too young to get a bookkeeper. Your journey isn't too new to start it the right way.

There are many Advisory firms in the online business brokerage space. True, not all are created equal, but you may have to determine that for yourself. I'm writing *The EXITpreneur's Playbook* on my own, not as a partner at Quiet Light. I want you to do what is best for you, and to connect with whomever feels right. And the only way to do that is to take action, reach out, and speak with someone.

ONE MORE STORY

Ethan's business sold for a million dollars plus inventory to a man named Jack. Within twelve months after buying it, Jack tripled the size of the business. They've stayed in touch since then, and the most recent update is that Jack is currently in a position to sell the business for $5 million.

The traditional mindset is filled with fears of missing out. It says Ethan should have waited and sold it himself later. It says Jack took advantage of Ethan's missed opportunity. It burrows down into our brains and keeps us feverishly building businesses far beyond our level of competence or comfort.

But Ethan is an EXITpreneur. He had a goal in mind. He worked down a path toward that goal and he achieved it, then he moved on to his next adventure—running the family business.

Perhaps, if he felt as though his family business could wait, he could have moved that goalpost another twelve months away. Jack came from the corporate world and was very good at building teams. It was Jack's skills that took the business to the next level. But Jack needed Ethan's solopreneur skills to get the business off the ground in the first place. They both won.

This isn't about how much you can extract. It's about a method that reliably achieves goals, both for you and for someone else.

That's the biggest reason we repeat. It's not just a way of making money—you can find ways of making money anywhere. This is a way to create purpose and meaning in the world, even if you're just selling widgets or writing about the next apocalypse. You're creating something for someone else. You're creating something bigger than you. Bigger than all of us.

You're an EXITpreneur now. Welcome to the team.

Ah, no, I am not done yet. YOU have to take some action now... just three simple (yeah, right) steps.

1. Set goals.
   A. How much will you sell for?
   B. When will you sell?
   C. How do you want to feel when you sell?
2. Calculate your SDE: Run your P&Ls and do your best at creating an add-back schedule and your SDE. If you need help, visit EXITpreneur.io.
   A. If you cannot run a monthly P&L, visit EXITpreneur.io/ Resources and I'll connect you with a superb bookkeeper or two.
3. How does your business fare in the Risk, Growth, Transferability, and Documentation areas? Be honest and look at them from a buyer's perspective, and review Chapter 4. And then fix what needs fixing. Leave it up to your buyer and they'll pay you less for your business.

In order to reverse engineer a path toward your goals, you have to know where you are today. Without this knowledge, you won't know how close or how far away you are from them.

The information in this book should help you understand how little details can add up to big value. But remember, you have just enough information to be dangerous (to yourself) now. You are an orange belt. Seek out a qualified Advisor that has built, bought, or sold their own online business and now helps others achieve their own goals as well.

Now I'm done.

ACKNOWLEDGMENTS

My fellow entrepreneurs: To the thousands I've spoken with over the last decade, your drive and passion have fueled and motivated me. Thank you for sharing your experiences and allowing me to help. You've helped me in return, and we're all in this together.

The Quiet Light team: It has been and continues to be an honor and a privilege to work with each and every one of you.

My wife and two boys: I am, without a doubt, a better human because of you. Thank you for loving, laughing, and lighting up my life.

My parents: You led by example, never said the word impossible, and allowed me to fail. Thank you for never giving up on your entrepreneur-in-the-making, all the way back to grade school!

My in-laws: Years ago, you gave me a paperweight with "Every Wall is a Door" on it. Thank you for the inspiration, understanding who I am and what drives me.

This book's interviewees: While the interviews did not make it into this book as planned, your ideas and inspiration are sprinkled throughout. Thank you for your time and dedication to helping make this book a reality.

Scribe Media: Seriously…brilliant business model that helps, helps, and helps some more. Oh, and Brannan…simply awesome.

ABOUT THE AUTHOR

JOE VALLEY is a serial entrepreneur, EXITpreneur, advisor, and partner at Quiet Light, one of the leading online-focused M&A firms in the world. He has built, bought, and sold over a half dozen companies of his own, and has helped thousands of online entrepreneurs achieve their goals. Joe holds a business degree from Northeastern University, is a Certified Mergers and Acquisitions Professional, and is a frequent guest expert in mastermind groups, on podcasts, and at events for online entrepreneurs throughout the world. He lives in North Carolina with his wife and two children.

For more on Joe, including resources to help you along your EXITpreneur journey, visit EXITpreneur.io.

Made in the USA
Columbia, SC
01 July 2021

41166614R00183